THINK CLEARLY AND ACT WITH FOCUS

FOR A MEANINGFUL LIFE

Marta Marques Villagra

V713 Villagra, Marta Marques
    Think clearly and act with focus – For a meaningful
life. 3. ed. / Marta Marques Villagra. São Paulo: Marta Villagra
System, 2024.
210 p.; 13,97x21,59.

ISBN: 978-65-89972-75-4
Includes bibliography.

1. Coaching; 2. TOC; 3. Purpose; 4. Focus; 5. Personal growth; 6.
Consciousness.

                      CDD: 370

ABOUT THE AUTHOR

Marta Villagra is an ICF (International Coaching Federation) member, certified by the ICI (Instituto de Coaching Integrado), and post-graduated in Teaching Methodologies. Guest speaker and lecturer in the United States, Brazil, and Israel.

She has experience developing executive coaching processes for over a decade in Brazil and abroad. She has clients in various expertise areas, including family business executives in succession processes, autonomous professionals, and young people, becoming an expert in using the thinking processes of the Theory of Constraints applied for personal growth.

Her passion is helping individuals think clearly about their reality, define a purpose, and generate the necessary change to obtain a meaningful life, utilizing their full potential.

Email: marta@martavillagrasystem.com
            marta@villagra.com.br
Instagram: martavillagracoaching
Facebook: Marta Villagra – Coaching
LinkedIn: martavillagra
www.martavillagrasystem.com
www.villagracoaching.com.br

To be happy is to live in congruence with your primary values without anything making you deviate from them. It's the freedom to make daily choices that address a greater purpose. It is realizing your contribution to the evolution of the world being who you are.

Marta Marques Villagra

To my parents, Maria Guedes Marques and Tarquínio Francisco Marques, who welcomed me with love in this life, responsible for forming my first values through example.

ACKNOWLEDGMENTS

Above all, I thank God for blessing my steps and choices, even when I was unaware of where they would take me. And for sustaining the core of my purpose: love of thy neighbor.

I thank Aureo Villagra for being my biggest supporter since we met in 1986, helping me fulfill myself in life. His words are from that time, in the dedication of a gift, the book 'There's no such place as far away' by Richard Bach: "Choose what you really want to do with your life and do it!"

Thank you, Aureo, above all, for the love, clarity of thought, and attitudes that I admire and impact my achievements, including my decision to write this book.

I am grateful to my children, Daniela and Mauro, for believing and supporting my professional path and as a mother, each in their own way, with technical help, participation, feedback, spontaneous hugs, smiles, and concerns. Aureo and I are happy to bring two people with integrity and value to the world.

I feel gratitude for all who took the precious time to read this book and contribute with their sincere and valuable feedback before it was published.

To the clients with whom I always grow through their personal and professional life experiences, thank you very much for your dedication and openness to growth. I wish you all a continually meaningful life.

To Dr. Goldratt and his family, thank you for the teachings and opportunity to "stand on the shoulders of giants to see further."

SUMÁRIO

I remember the scene vividly. I had asked Marta to be a guest speaker at the closing of the Goldratt Holistic Management program in São Paulo. The program participants ranged from directors and managers of several companies around Brazil. They had learned and applied the Theory of Constraints (TOC) principles in their companies for over six months. I wanted them to understand how universal these principles are—applicable to advancing organizational performance and personal life.

I knew that Marta had integrated the use of TOC into her coaching practices. I knew her clients' results in their personal and professional lives. She was my natural choice to share this "soft side" of using TOC. She was nervous and didn't want to disappoint.

And she didn't disappoint. Not even a little bit.

The group captured her every word as she explained how the same principles we apply to business could be used for ourselves. And she did it not only with logic but with all the love, lightness, feeling, and authenticity that is Marta.

• Make your purpose and goals clear – if you don't define them, then even the best of plans leaves it to chance whether or not you will live a meaningful and fulfilling life.

•	Identify the constraint – the only thing standing in the way between today and living your purpose, achieving so much more of your goal.

•	Find out what to do to overcome the constraint – become your obstacle remover!

•	And then do it! Act, learn from what you do and the results you generate, making corrections along the way. Remembering that in the end, it's about the journey.

In this book, Marta brings the same authenticity to her subject as she did that day in São Paulo. She captures you in her own story. She shares insights gained in the process she uses with her coaching clients to help them help themselves. And she introduces you to each step of its process, using case examples inspired by her clients and her life.

Martha's mantra is "Think clearly, act with focus" to lead a fuller and more meaningful life. Your process helps you in just that.

If you want to gain insights into a process that guides you into unlocking what a more meaningful and fulfilling life is, this book is for you.

Lisa Scheinkopf

INTRODUCTION

Every system has inherent simplicity, no matter how complex it may seem!

I first heard this principle about ten years ago, at a very proper and unique time in my life. This paradigm shift brought me hope because if reality is simple, solutions must be, too. There was a thinking process to unravel this simplicity and see it.

This scientific approach generates growth, stability, and harmony in the business environment. It has extended its applications to different industries for almost forty years and reached human development. It's about thinking to get clarity on reality and find the best change solutions and significant improvement.

We are individuals involved in many roles, contexts, and areas of interest. In this way, throughout life, we embrace responsibilities and assume different attributions, problems, and passions.

We live searching! We seek to establish ourselves through our results, image, challenges, and achievements. In this constant search, we disperse our attention among many choices, and, in the end, it seems that the hours and efforts spent are still insufficient to gain the long-awaited personal fulfillment as a reward.

It seems to be a complex reality. That's how I used to live.

And I was there, listening, thinking, applying the tools, and learning because, typically, when we are involved in a complex situation, we naturally believe that improvement solutions must be equally complex. That was the first paradigm I had to break.

In fact, according to the scientific approach, the more complex a reality is, the simpler the way it is governed. Seeing the reality and its inherent simplicity gave me the power to change it for the better. Once I understood this principle, I started a new way of thinking.

Theory of Constraints

I was living a stable reality when, by sheer chance, I was introduced to the Theory of Constraints, known worldwide as TOC. Its principles have become a part of my personal and professional life.

But what is this way of thinking anyway? And where did it come from?

Almost four decades ago, TOC was launched with the book The Goal, an approach to business management written as a novel by the Israeli Physicist Dr. Eliyahu Goldratt. The Goal quickly became an international bestseller and is still a reference worldwide.

TOC revolutionized business thinking, allowing companies to achieve results quickly. It is a management philosophy based on logic that supports understanding reality and its interconnected components.

With success achieved, Dr. Eli Goldratt and his team began developing TOC applications in various areas. An international community of professionals and applications emerged, further expanding this knowledge.

TOC consists of a set of processes and tools that organize thinking through the logic of cause and effect while considering emotion and intuition, attributing them to clear verbalization and meaning. Its approach helps validate our assumptions and identify those that prevent us from thinking clearly.

Personal growth

What do you really want to achieve or change in your life?

What prevents you from living your inherent potential and achieving what you want?

Answering these questions would not be possible without the tools and processes to help me reach assertive answers and discover precisely what to change.

Our way of thinking gives rise to the reality that surrounds us. A program based on TOC allowed me to make essential changes in my personal and professional life. But far beyond that, I learned consistent principles that have contributed to my life since then, bringing more clarity and simplicity to how I think, feel, decide, and act.

At this stage, I identified an excellent opportunity to use these thinking processes to enhance the coaching industry. A coach's central role is to help people rationalize the current context and facilitate improvement decisions for a new reality. I soon became convinced that the TOC thinking processes could bring clarity and harmony through logic.

At first glance, the term 'logic' sounded cold because it didn't seem to consider emotions or feelings. But contrary to what I could imagine, there is a logic behind our feelings and way of thinking. We interpret facts and attitudes with a greater or lesser degree of logic.

The scientific method teaches us to challenge the assumptions underlying our emotions and actions. Without this critical examination, we risk living in dissonance with our expectations of reality, hindering our growth and preventing us from seizing better opportunities. Therefore, employing logic helps uncover the truths that often elude us at first glance.

Applying the Theory of Constraints (TOC) to my life taught me how logic could help me understand the facts and feelings that troubled me and prevented me from realizing my inherent potential. Gaining clarity through logical thinking was exactly what I needed to initiate the desired changes and achieve a meaningful life.

The impact of these thinking processes in helping individuals achieve their goals extends beyond obtaining results. It makes them adopt the mindset that will govern their lives.

After applying TOC in my personal life, researching, and practicing with people of diverse cultures and nationalities for over ten years, I developed the MVS Method—Marta Villagra System.

My objective with this book is to introduce the MVS method for personal and professional growth, utilizing the principles of TOC as a differentiator. These practical principles are accessible to every reality and induce a new way of thinking that leads to a more meaningful life.

I present the method in a simplified way, with examples based on real cases, so readers with different backgrounds can capture the basic idea I am sharing.

CHAPTER I – HOW TOC IMPACTED MY LIFE

"To each their own"

Our development process starts the day we are conceived. As babies, we begin to present our first profile traits. And at a young age, it is already possible to observe how we respond and react differently to people and situations.

Our characteristics and emotions emerge as we experience life. The circumstances of our environment and the people around us contribute to these experiences.

That's awesome!

As a child, I used to say, "To each to their own". It was my way of acknowledging what I perceived about people in general, and that phrase always came to me in different moments. Perhaps I already suspected that people were different and acted their way not needing to be equals.

Later, my interest arose when I developed a final paper for specialization on teaching-learning methodologies—this time, "to each to their own" in academic practice. I set my study based on a humanistic and student-centered learning foundation, incorporating a behavioral analysis tool.

The purpose was to provide an understanding of the different behavioral profiles of students and teachers so that teaching strategies can be managed, and knowledge acquisition facilitated through effective interpersonal relationships.

We perceive reality differently and are motivated differently. In addition, we exert influence and have socially distinct roles in how we contribute to teams. Therefore, knowledge of behavioral profiles can impact the success of the teaching-learning process.

After a few decades, this phrase is still present and validates the importance of self-knowledge, a starting point in personal development.

I have always considered it essential to have a way to accelerate people's process of discovering who they are and what they are looking for in their lives. I understood that it was necessary for them to seek what makes sense for themselves and define a life purpose in which they feel personally and professionally fulfilled.

My challenge

I had not gone through any professional development process until adulthood, and something substantial was needed to improve my journey.

In 2001, I was a wife and mother of two, as well as a teacher, a businesswoman, and financially stable. Like everyone else, I held many roles and have always strived to achieve the best results from my efforts.

Without realizing it, we assume various responsibilities throughout life and as opportunities arise, striving to find personal and professional satisfaction. I lived what appeared to be a harmonious life; however, in reality, l had a vague awareness of my purpose. In the eyes of others, everything seemed perfectly in order and guided by the luck and blessings that life had bestowed upon me; I continued with my daily routine.

But I lived with a feeling of discomfort with myself. Eager to find professional and personal fulfillment, I moved from one opportunity to another. I took new courses while struggling to adapt to the time spent at home, raising children, having a family, and a social life. But something was bothering me internally. I didn't feel like I was utilizing my potential, as if I was letting time pass.

I've learned that investing time in defining the problem speeds up achieving effective change. Naturally, when we find ourselves in uncomfortable situations, we look directly for solutions to alleviate the discomfort. We barely focus on really understanding the problem we are trying to solve.

Today, I know how self-knowledge, the awareness of a personal purpose, and the right mindset can influence individual fulfillment. Now, I understand that I lacked a greater awareness of my inner and outer universe. I lived at the mercy of circumstances and followed only instincts, with no vision of the scope of growth.

Without a clear conscience, we can easily fall into a state of personal dissatisfaction. We look for reasons for this, and we can't find them. Everything looks as it should, or it seems like someone else's fault. We quickly attribute responsibility to others or the conditions we find ourselves in as if nothing depended on our choices.

In this dissatisfaction, we look for solutions and act in a creative short-circuit mode. We make new decisions, and as we execute them, we see that they do not bring what we are looking for, or they may bring temporary results with new undesirable effects.

Consequently, we often try to change reality and give up on projects, courses, jobs, countries, partners, collaborators, and sometimes even ourselves. We take other paths and face the same dilemmas and conflicts as before. Does this sound familiar?

What was I about to discover: What blocks you from living your true potential?

A journey from the inside to the outside

A singular moment came along: a sudden change and health crisis that had me using a cane for six months due to severely herniated discs, culminating in emergency lumbar spine surgery. But there was an invitation waiting for me.

My husband, Aureo Villagra, Global Partner and CEO of the South America operation of Goldratt Consulting, initiated the invitation to participate in a program created by Eli Goldratt and led by Dr. Alan Barnard, a TOC expert.

It was in 2011 in San Jose, California. Twenty days before the departure, an emergency surgery nearly interrupted our plans. But I persisted, and we left. My steps were slower and perhaps more conscious this time, but they took me further.

Thus began a new trajectory in my life.

I learned I needed to get a complete picture of my reality before choosing to change. From this point of view, it was possible to locate the main causes and conflicts that prevented the situation from improving significantly. This principle of the scientific method contributed significantly to improving the reality in which I found myself.

I needed clarity on what to change, as my earlier attempts only led to temporary improvements. Different opportunities didn't seem enough to achieve my professional and personal growth. Worse, each time I made a new decision, I faced the same feeling of stagnation after the initial euphoria of accomplishment had passed. All I needed was a better understanding of my reality and how it worked.

With TOC thinking processes, I verbalized the undesirable effects in different areas of my life. I understood how many effects were interconnected in a cause-and-effect logic from that vision.

As I learned to verbalize these effects correctly, something significant emerged. I finally understood my truths. The method allowed me to move from victimization to dominance, realizing I was building a change process. Understanding reality was the only way to identify what needed to change. I could transform what was just a sensation into something concrete and understand the logic of cause and effect that governed my life.

The program used to take place in a country, with participants from all over the world in every edition. Seeing people from different cultures in this edition doing the same with the help of a professional made me realize that we are not in this world by chance and that I was not the only one desiring to achieve personal fulfillment.

After those five days, I was impressed by the thinking processes of TOC. It sparked my interest in the principles and tools governing decisions and regulating emotions, bringing clarity and harmony to a new life ahead. But I needed more time to fully apply it, as something important was about to happen.

Unusual decision

We decided to stay in the United States longer to restart the process. We drove from San Jose to Las Vegas, where, by the irony of fate, we found peace on the twentieth floor of a hotel overlooking the churning reality beneath our feet.

I restarted the process, applying the methodology more deeply to obtain the correct verbalization. Due to my post-operative condition, I was accompanied by my Aureo Villagra, who had already mastered the TOC thinking processes in a business environment. It was a genuine inner journey. So, I turned off the focus on applying the reasoning techniques I had been enchanted with and let myself be guided by an expert to delve into my truths, feelings, and intentions with full attention.

Figure 1 – Reviewing the process in deeply

Having completed the first phase of the process, we used the tool Current Reality Tree to organize my context at that time. The scientific principle of thinking clearly came through the convergence of various effects connected to a root cause.

When analyzing the current reality, I identified three areas of life with undesirable effects that bothered me and led to my dissatisfaction: professional, family, and social contribution areas. Careful not to blame anyone or attribute my undesirable effects to speculated causes, I transcribed the feelings and thoughts I had previously been unable to express.

One of my discoveries was that I used to be fully present in my children's education. At the same time, this diverted my attention from professional decisions, making me feel unprepared for new steps.

This situation triggered other undesirable effects that impacted the areas of family and social contribution. I didn't feel productive, which raised doubts about my ability, and, therefore, I didn't feel like a good role model for my children. This vicious cycle generated new effects.

I was always there when my children came home from their various activities. While this was often fulfilling, it also created a dependency on me, which could be frustrating. I also felt I was missing out on my social connections and groups. It seemed like I couldn't find a balance, as each decision or choice I made left me unsatisfied.

Nowadays, I realize that my values used to dictate these "lacks" or undesirable effects. The process guided me on a journey of discovery and self-knowledge, where I could glimpse my true life purpose for the first time.

The following figure represents the connection of undesirable effects converging to the root cause, the main factor to be changed.

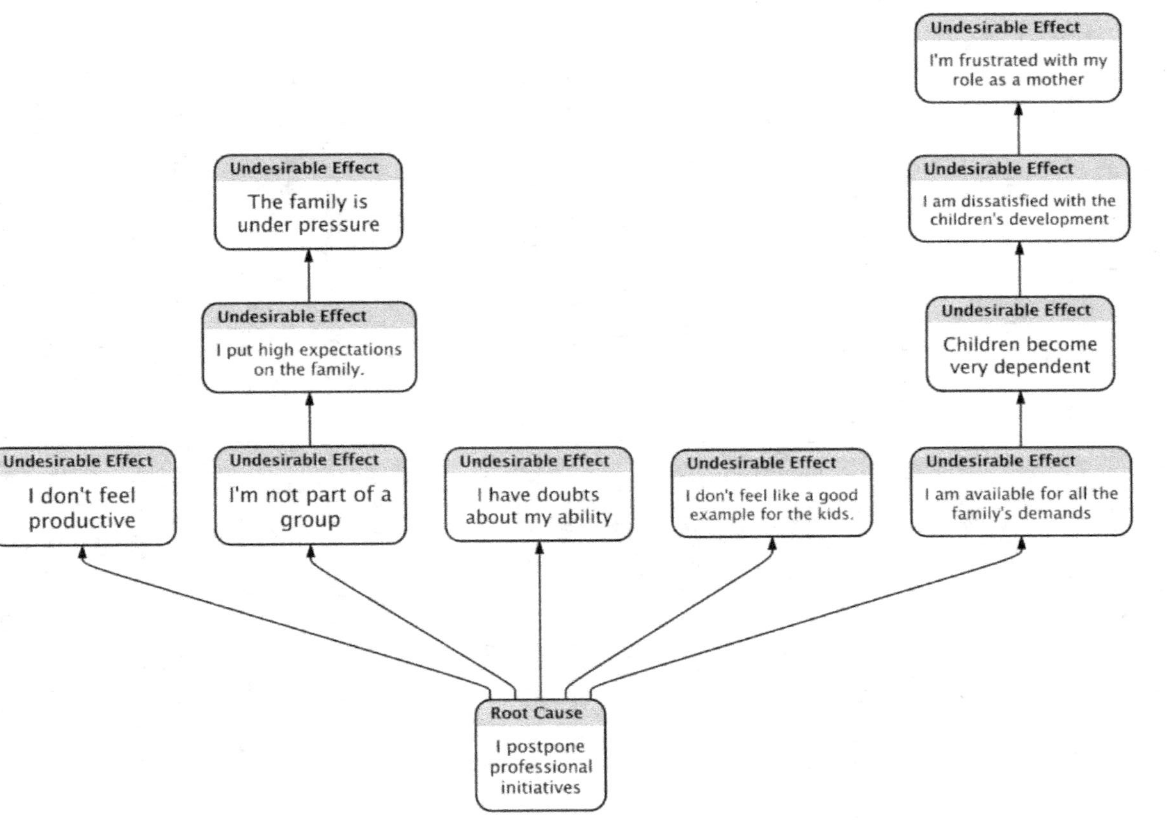

Figure 2 - My Current Reality Tree

I discovered the logic behind every context in which I lived. So, I learned the first TOC pillar described in the introduction of this book:

Every system has inherent simplicity, no matter how complex it may seem!

I understood that I would not have to act on each effect. Solving the root conflict would generate the change needed for the desired future reality.

How I solved my problem

The leading cause of my limited growth was a dilemma: after all, why hadn't I taken steps towards satisfactorily advancing my career? My personal growth depended on two valid needs that demanded opposing actions.

To grow professionally, I needed to take advantage of opportunities that arose, regardless of the conditions. However, I wanted to guarantee good results, so I searched for ideal conditions.

The dilemma became clear—the resistance to thinking I was never prepared enough prevented me from advancing in the professional area. In addition to not being clear about the real professional purpose, something prevented me from acting. Through the TOC process, I gained a broader view of my reality and identified which undesirable effects stemming from my core conflict.

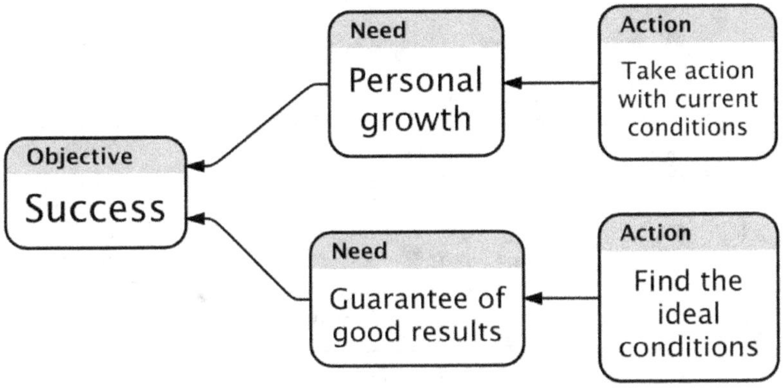

Figure 3 – My core conflict

After questioning the assumptions that supported my conflict, we found a win-win solution that would address both valid needs: seizing opportunities and ensuring good results.

The solution came from two concepts I learned from TOC: acting with current conditions and recognizing what might be good enough to start. Second, implementing the POOGI process—Process of Ongoing Improvement. This technique commonly used in TOC consists of learning from experience. By identifying new constraints that may threaten the plan. We will face new realities when we act quickly toward the path of change. Therefore, feedback is needed to adjust actions and undo new obstacles.

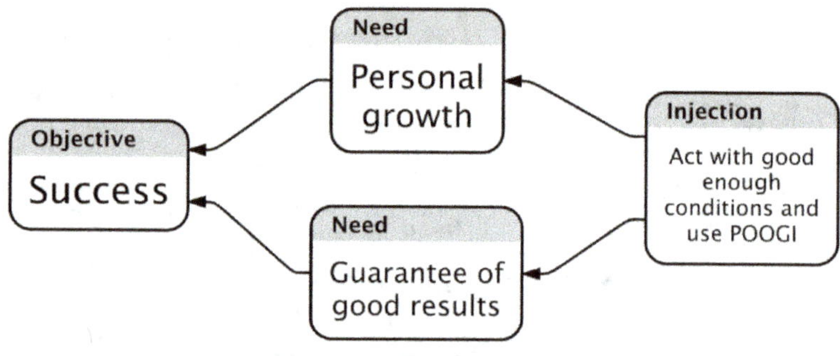

Figure 4 – The injection

This solution, called an 'injection' in TOC, was applied to solve my core conflict. Like every elegant solution, it looks elementary after being verbalized!

Thus emerged the Future Reality Tree, where undesirable effects turned into desirable ones. It would only take a few additional small injections to ensure a successful implementation.

I would no longer be fully present for my children by taking professional initiatives. Still, I would simultaneously feel like a good example and reduce their dependence by getting their cooperation. It would make me proud of my role as a mother.

By taking on extra commitments, I created plans to maintain family interaction and organize a schedule with a buffer time to avoid stress. On the other hand, taking professional initiatives included being part of a business group with which I could grow and contribute. The unproductiveness and the doubt about my ability were reversed into feelings of personal and professional fulfillment and satisfaction.

Although minor side effects emerged during this experience, the continuous improvement process, supported by professional follow-up and prompt feedback, facilitated the desired growth in harmony.

Figure 5 - My Future Reality Tree

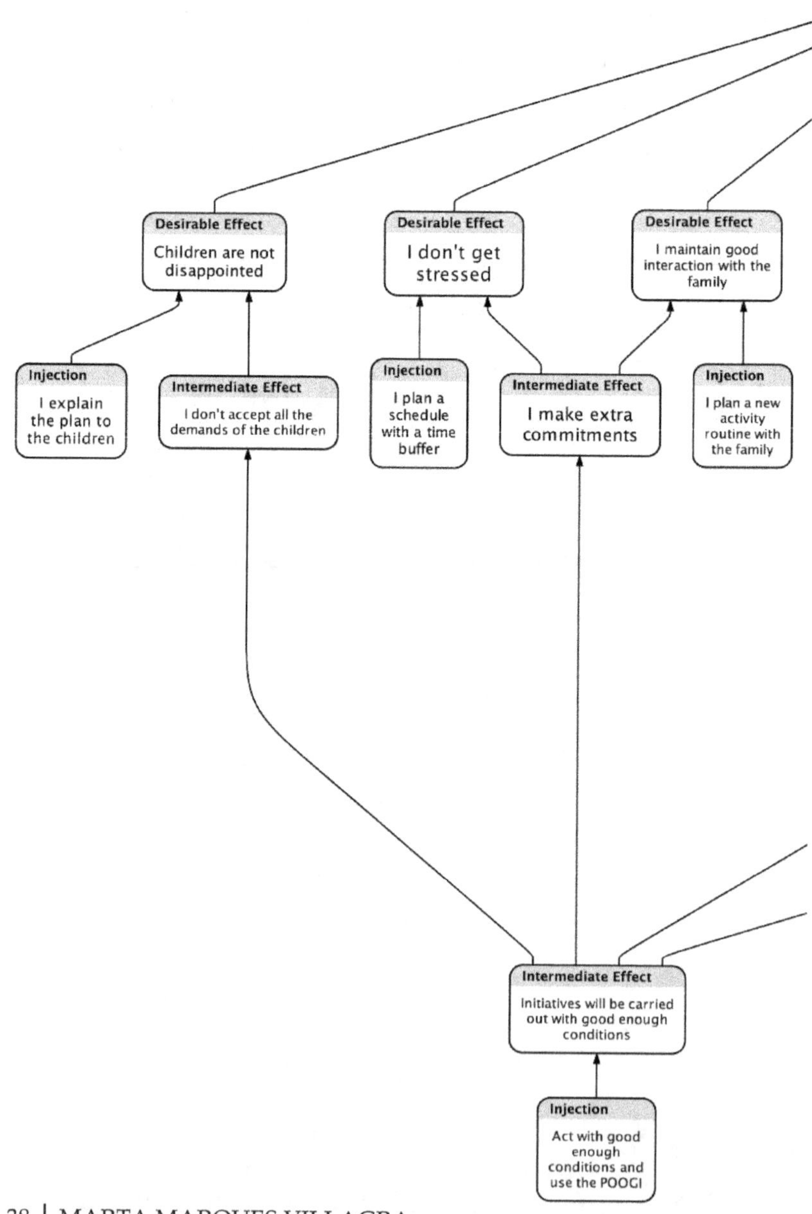

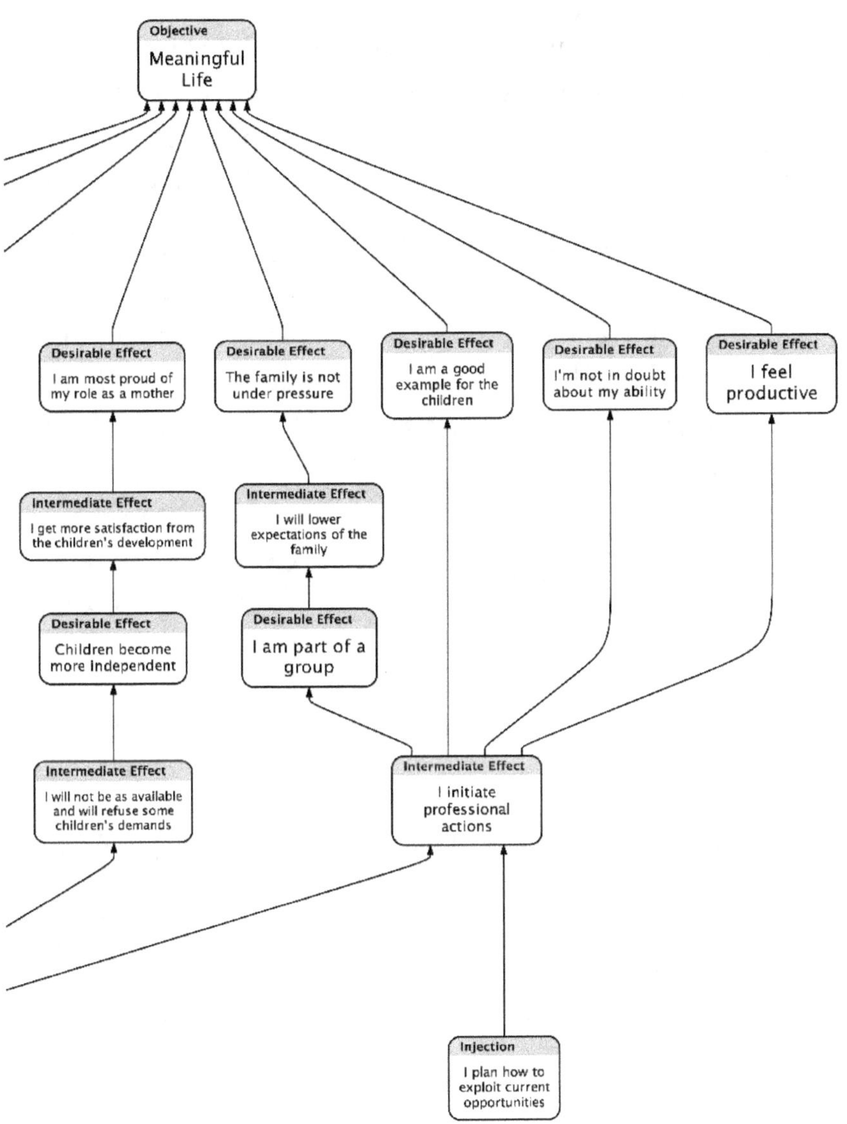

Objective
Meaningful Life

Desirable Effect
I am most proud of my role as a mother

Desirable Effect
The family is not under pressure

Desirable Effect
I am a good example for the children

Desirable Effect
I'm not in doubt about my ability

Desirable Effect
I feel productive

Intermediate Effect
I get more satisfaction from the children's development

Intermediate Effect
I will lower expectations of the family

Desirable Effect
Children become more independent

Desirable Effect
I am part of a group

Intermediate Effect
I will not be as available and will refuse some children's demands

Intermediate Effect
I initiate professional actions

Injection
I plan how to exploit current opportunities

Even though we are aware of the solution we must implement, obstacles can often threaten the success of the plan. Therefore, we define intermediate objectives and actions to overcome the obstacles.

A roadmap was established by identifying the conflict and finding a solution that eliminated it. Actions were defined in a logical sequence, considering necessary conditions and intermediate objectives, bringing security and clarity in the direction of my purpose.

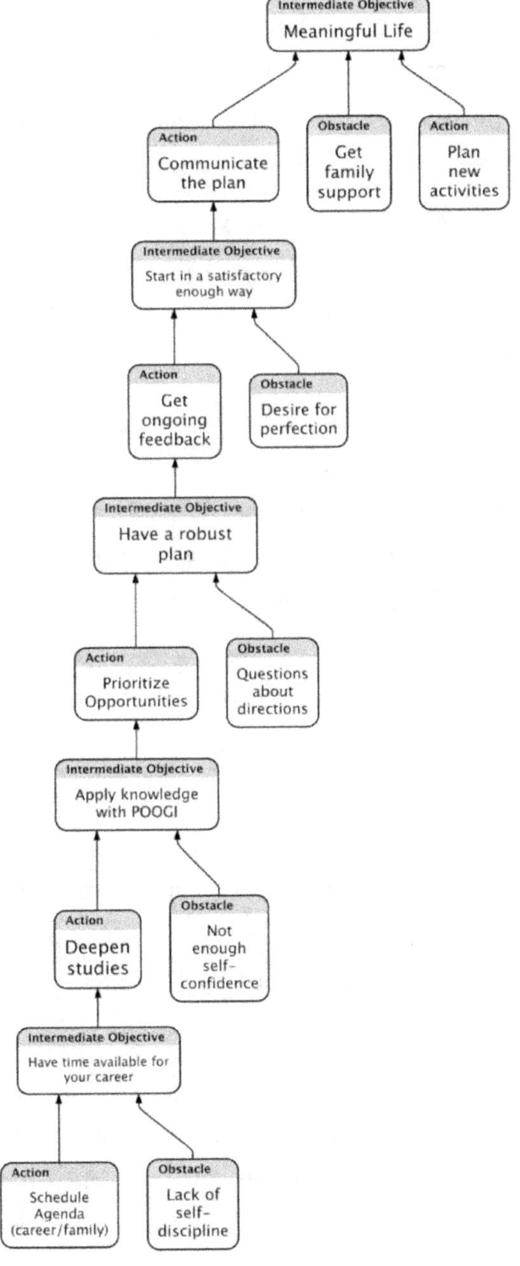

Figure 6 - My Roadmap

This organized process raised a new way of thinking, expanding my vision and allowing me to see my reality and act on it. At that moment, I visualized the path leading me to live a new reality with purpose.

I started to understand that the methodology was based on a unique way of thinking, which inspired my professional slogan in coaching: "Think clearly and act with focus."

Eli Goldratt used to say that management attention is the optimal constraint that impedes an organization's or a person's performance. Once the focus for significant improvement has been established, whether at an institutional, corporate, or personal level, it is necessary to identify what may hinder or limit our attention to ensure effective execution.

New decisions or opportunities quickly interrupt or influence us. Managing attention often means consciously saying no to ourselves, others, or situations. The focus is on learning what to stop doing rather than knowing what to do. I see that sometimes this also applies to what to think about and what to stop thinking about.

We can manage our thoughts to harmonize our emotions and, consequently, our reactions. This helps us analyze our thoughts and emotions better and seek to understand the thoughts and emotions of those around us.

As the renewed author Daniel Goleman proposed, I realized how the logic of cause and effect could contribute to developing emotional intelligence. We begin to recognize and deal better with our own emotions like we start to acknowledge and seek to understand others' emotions through logic.

Our thinking is seriously considered, as it originates our emotions. I observe this through my own experience and others as I apply the thinking processes of the theory of constraints.

During my initiation into TOC, I immediately fell in love with the principles that supported the methodology. Its structure and tools made it possible to recognize conflicts and find solutions, verbalize undesirable effects, and challenge wrong assumptions in a way that harmonized emotions. Thus, feelings of motivation and hope gradually replaced feelings of dissatisfaction. A new reality was becoming possible.

Facing inconsistencies is the raw material for generating disruptive solutions. I was excited about making new decisions as I became aware of what was blocking me before—the root cause, the core problem. Acting on it would generate all the consequences of significant improvement.

My problem was regarding taking new initiatives in the professional space. What would I put at risk by taking action? My deep-rooted values were also at risk in other areas, especially in the family. I could see clearly how to maintain them, while at the same time, I went into the action itself.

After identifying a comprehensive global solution rather than a local one, a series of measures were logically implemented to mitigate negative impacts in other areas. The solution guided the strategic injections that restored harmony.

I felt as though my life was a locomotive that had just restarted its engines. It seemed obvious what to do, and a feeling of certainty replaced that of insecurity. Everything was done consciously, and all the implications of the change were taken seriously. Thus, we could anticipate other undesired effects that may come from the change and thus take steps to ensure everything went well.

Armed with this new awareness and comprehensive documentation, I took action alongside my husband, Aureo, who played a pivotal role in this renewal opportunity. This approach fostered credibility through the guidance of a professional coach who conducts a thinking process by asking pertinent questions, actively listening to answers, and encouraging clear and precise verbalization.

Helping others

After going through the process, I was invited to help assist the program the following year. This time, in Tel Aviv, I assisted the participants' groups and helped them apply the methodology for their personal growth. In 2013, I helped organize the program in Rio de Janeiro, Brazil. We had participants from all over the world, and now more Brazilians could attend.

As an assistant, I guided individuals from diverse cultural backgrounds in using TOC tools that enabled them to articulate their goals, identify undesirable effects, and resolve conflicts. This process helped them discover optimal solutions to realize their potential and craft a more meaningful life plan.

The factors that inhibit an individual from realizing more of their potential vary widely, just as life goals do. I witnessed various cases, from the most typical, such as the search for self-esteem through weight loss, to the most atypical, such as overcoming one's strength limits by climbing a dangerous mountain or ending hunger in one's homeland.

In all cases, undesirable effects were connected, and dilemmas were identified. By eliminating these dilemmas, new disruptive actions emerged, unlocking the way forward. Roadmaps come to facilitate tracking and ensure the desired change.

Through my experience, I demonstrated that this scientific approach to thinking was accessible to people of diverse origins and ages. I also discovered that pursuing a more meaningful life was a common goal, affirming that I was not alone in this challenge.

It is interesting how logic-based thinking accounts for emotions and can drive action, thereby efficiently fostering mastery over our lives. We often delay decisions or resort to shortcuts that divert us from what we want, either because we fail to see reality clearly or because we avoid challenging our thinking.

After this experience, I continued my TOC studies and received additional coaching training. After six years of practice, I developed the MVS System, applying the Theory of Constraints for personal and professional growth.

CHAPTER II – HOW I USED TOC MINDSET

It's all part of the way we think.

Carl Rogers, the psychologist who developed Humanistic Psychology, already theorized that people don't have problems. The problem lies in their way of thinking. How we think and the conclusions we reach about situations determine our emotions and reactions to what we experience.

For this reason, thinking logically helps us analyze situations more accurately, allowing us to see more clearly and make choices that are better aligned with reality.

Driven by this concern and interest, Eli Goldratt developed the TOC to teach the world to think logically and reveal simple solutions for complex situations.

This approach increases our power of influence, enabling us to solve problems and improve our emotional and cognitive state, that is, our perception of ourselves, others, and the diverse contexts in which we are involved.

Most people believe that when they are unsatisfied with something, they must change everything that does not seem good. Therefore, they resort to half-measures or radical steps to escape the unfavorable context. Their focus is either too dispersed or too localized, often resulting in poor outcomes.

We solve problems in isolation without knowing how they will impact the whole environment. The TOC approach teaches us to think clearly about reality before simply setting out to solve a problem. Some tools facilitate logical thinking to understand reality better, whether on a personal or organizational level.

All we need is to think clearly.

Three strategic questions in TOC underpin this process of significant improvement:

1- What to change?

2- What to change to?

3- How to cause the change?

According to Dr. Goldratt, every improvement requires a change, but not every change causes an improvement. That is why these three questions deserve particular attention with the support of adequate and well-conducted tools. Applying the TOC-based process fosters a new mindset that helps people gain clarity and focus on thinking and acting.

The principles that govern our thinking compound what we call a mindset. Our brain takes milliseconds to process external stimuli, arising thoughts and thus our reactions to them. Therefore, adopting a mindset that gives us confidence fosters the success of our plans. It enlarges the vision of opportunities. We can educate our thinking to protect ourselves from unfavorable responses to situations, decisions, and relationships.

Humans are easily compelled to act on assumptions that do not match the facts. Other times, we make impulsive decisions that do not bring satisfactory results. We judge facts and people too quickly, missing opportunities instead of generating growth and harmony.

Our way of thinking can leverage our lives or limit them.

TOC Pillars

Once we are convinced of the principles that sustain it, we can develop a mindset that favors our lives. We can exercise it and observe the improvement in our results, the quality of our choices, our relationships, and the changes we make to live a full life.

Dr. Goldratt organized the basic principles of TOC into four pillars, which form the way of thinking to achieve a fulfilling life.

Figure 7 - The TOC Pillars

Inherent Simplicity

During the COVID-19 pandemic, a journalist said, "The situation is very complex and requires complex solutions." It is typical for people to look for sophisticated solutions to complex situations and expect effectiveness. However, the more complex the solutions, the less effective they tend to be in terms of results, as it is easy to lose focus on what needs to be done to generate overall improvement. In addition, complex solutions can cause unpredictable effects, for which we quickly lose control.

The scientific method proposes just the opposite. Figuring out the one factor restricting the system from functioning simplifies the solution.

Whenever a problem threatens a complex system, all actions must align in the same direction towards a single simple solution, as this will strengthen and protect the entire system. Therefore, to significantly improve a complex situation, the solution must be simple and applied in a way that does not threaten other essential areas. For this reason, the focus is a word with a powerful meaning. It emphasizes focusing on what needs to be done rather than everything that could be improved.

When we implement several solutions simultaneously to improve a highly complex situation, we lose focus, making it difficult to achieve significant results and potentially causing more undesirable effects.

Whenever we work with complex systems such as a nation, a community, a company, our home, or our personal life, we need to clearly see the interconnectedness between the current effects and unravel the inherent simplicity in how these systems work.

We can clarify our reality and focus on what will make an impact. Once we learn and practice, this way of thinking can help relieve stress and anxiety and improve our confidence in decision-making and problem-solving.

Dilemmas have a solution

A dilemma is established whenever there is a clash of interests between two parties or contradictory actions to achieve a common objective. Whenever two parties are in conflict, it means that each side needs to be threatened by two different actions. As they are opponents, one action harms the performance of the other and vice versa.

Dilemmas can occur between two departments of a company, between two partners, between husband and wife, between two brothers, and between friends. However, they exist because we must meet two valid needs to solve a problem.

In some situations, the choice becomes tough because there are two equally necessary actions, each satisfying a different valid need but complementary to achieving a common objective. Sometimes, one action prevents the other from co-occurring. When choosing one of the actions, something important is lost.

In TOC, conflicts between two people or dilemmas regarding two contradictory decisions are solved by the same thinking process, leading to a win-

win solution that respects the common objective and satisfies complementary needs.

The most exciting thing is that this technique of identifying and resolving dilemmas can solve common problems among people and even generate innovative and unusual ideas.

Dilemmas are the raw material we need to discover better solutions and, thus, maintain harmony and growth.

How do we recognize a major conflict?

A. There is a common goal between the two sides.

B. The needs of each side are valid.

C. Actions taken to satisfy these needs threaten the needs of each party. Here lies the conflict.

If this is the context, one thing is sure: there is a solution to the dilemma. The common objective is a necessary condition. It is required to validate the needs that lead to the achievement of this objective. Once this is done, we must validate the actions satisfying these needs. Then comes the time to challenge the assumptions that support this conflict: what we think leads us to these needs and actions. Challenging assumptions is a thinking skill used to unravel inconsistencies in the reality of the facts and leads us to discover solutions that may have been hidden.

Therefore, whenever there is a dilemma in our personal or professional life, we must identify which inconsistency sustains it. The scientific approach says that there are no contradictions in reality. All we need is to understand the dilemma and challenge the assumptions that support it, leading to realizing actions or paradigm-changing that eliminate the dilemma and recover harmony in the system.

The application technique itself will be presented in the next chapter. For now, remember that 'every dilemma has a solution.'

People are good

Blaming people is not effective. Once, at a major client of Goldratt Consulting, Dr. Goldratt was asked if he believed people were good. He replied that he didn't know, but he found that they performed better when he developed solutions based on this assumption rather than when he blamed them. Therefore, he assumed that people are good, and a win-win solution might always exist.

Starting from the assumption that people are good leads us to understand what motivates them when they do something out of the ordinary or beyond our expectations.

People are different and have divergent perspectives and needs. We tend to judge and blame too quickly, which generates resistance and stagnation. Practicing empathy and persuasion to promote growth would be more effective.

What facilitates interpersonal connection in adverse situations is understanding how others think. If we defend our point of view without actively listening to others, there will be no connection or collaboration. In doing so, we may discover that we were the ones who were mistaken, as we did not possess all the necessary information. In this way, we will be generating opportunities for improvement. Whether in the family environment, community, or corporate environment, employing this principle improves the quality of our relationships, collaborates with better solutions, and opens pathways.

Never say I know

Many TOC experts characterize this pillar as the inherent potential that can be unlocked through the TOC thinking processes. If we think we already know everything about a situation, we stop thinking and block the possibility of creating something new.

Dr. Goldratt said that every situation and system could be substantially improved, no matter how good or bad it initially is.

He also said that "not even the sky is the limit".

According to the Theory of Constraints, there is always potential for significant improvement in every context. What may seem impossible at first glance constitutes an ambitious goal to explore. Questioning our assumptions is the key to reaching a much better reality.

There are two critical questions about leveraging an ambitious goal:

1- What is very difficult or even impossible, but if it weren't, would it change everything?

2- It is very difficult, unless….?

In critical situations, mainly when the outcome depends on a decision or a way of acting, we tend to assume ideas based on previous experiences or our interpretations and judgments about facts and people. Believing that we already know can cause inconsistencies between what we expect and what we get. We miss great opportunities when we close ourselves off to what we are not seeing or close ourselves off because we think we already know.

Dr. Goldratt often used the term 'humble arrogant': We must be arrogant enough to believe that we can improve any situation, yet humble enough to accept that we don't know everything. There is always more to learn.

This pillar bears a similarity to the 'growth mindset' explained by psychologist and author Carol Dweck in her book Mindset – The New Psychology of Success. The author describes how new experiences are viewed as learning and changing. If we fail in a particular life situation, we have the opportunity to find out what we should change. And that is positive. On the other hand, if we succeed, we must also remain open to accepting that situations can change and be willing to understand when it is time to relearn. If we always think we already know, we stop thinking - which limits our growth or the improvement of a system in which we are involved, and other people are equally involved.

'Never say you know' induces what we call continuous improvement. In TOC, there is a thinking technique that, when applied, promotes growth and prevents setbacks. These are the five focusing steps.

The 5 Focusing Steps

The TOC proposes five steps that describe what focus means in a systemic view:

1- Identify the constraint

2- Decide how to exploit the constraint

3- Subordinate everything else to the constraint

4- Elevate the constraint

5- Review everything to prevent inertia from becoming the constraint (go back to step 1)

I consider these steps a way of living the limitless potential of a company, an institution, a family, or a person.

An exciting analogy used in the TOC approach is the chain. When a chain breaks, it always fails at the weakest link. It is the same in life or our company. No matter how good we are, there will always be an aspect, a factor, or a critical link more susceptible to ruptures or setbacks, which can damage the system. Finding that link and applying the focusing steps guarantees extraordinary results rather than mediocre ones.

While writing this book, I noticed that a pandemic is taking its toll. Many people and companies were impacted; some were more prepared because they strengthened their weakest links and gave themselves opportunities to hold firm and emerge from the crisis.

Our world is dynamic; reality has never been so susceptible to uncertainties and drastic changes. Therefore, being attentive and focusing on continuous improvement can be extremely useful in good times and in adversity.

Thinking clearly and acting with focus are phases of development created based on the principles of TOC and will be exposed in the following chapters. Remembering that TOC teaches us to always look at reality, understand its simplicity, and act on what is needed, unlocking inherent potential.

The MVS Process

Throughout my coaching career, I encountered people eager to improve some aspects of their lives. Most of the time, these people sought improvement in their relationships or professional growth. Going through the process was an opportunity to understand their reality and define a purpose.

The willingness to grow and the humility to accept that something needs to be changed in how they deal with situations and their way of thinking are necessary for the advancement and success of the process.

I encountered people who were clear about what they wanted to change about themselves and recognized their limitations, including self-criticism and self-assessment. But why didn't they act and change what they needed? What they needed was a new way of thinking.

People seek support so that they are understood and receive support to organize their thoughts and improve the feelings inherent to their complaints about themselves and their reality. All they seek is social, emotional, and financial satisfaction in general. But what is the reason for not being able to change their reality? Lack of clarity.

People usually seek clarity because blurred vision caused by negative emotions resulting from distorted thoughts of reality makes life challenging to resolve.

The missing leverage factor is acting on what is needed. But as dynamic beings, we naturally rely on our intuition and immediately spring into action. However, learning to think clearly could add significant value.

This opportunity provides purpose and solutions to dilemmas that were not seen before.

Acquiring clarity about current reality motivates us to realize what we want and elucidates our purpose in life.

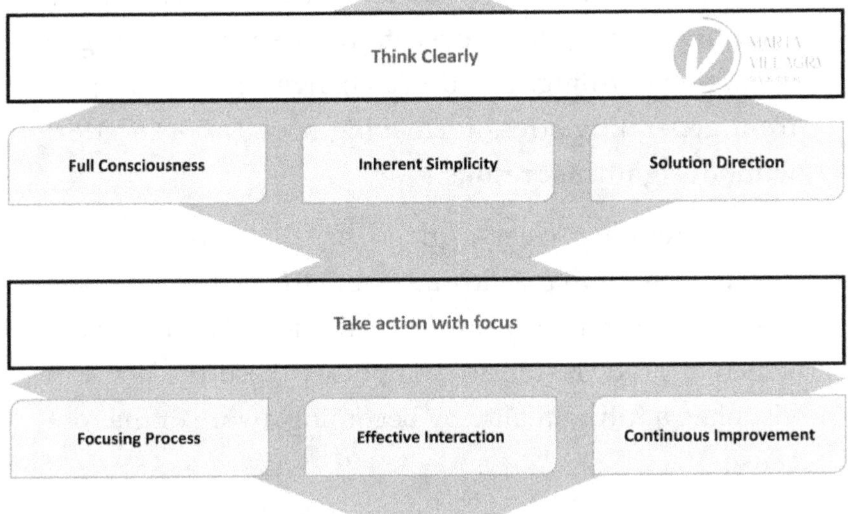

Figure 8 - The MVS System

Why think clearly?

When we try to change our reality without thinking clearly, we risk investing much effort and time only to have temporary or unsatisfactory results, and reality does not change.

It also occurs in all kinds of companies and businesses. Good people with the best intentions create systems or processes to fix each problem but do not focus on what matters most to improve.

A strong effort to do too many things results in a lack of focus and motivation. The common thought is,

"We did everything we could..." but the problem lies right there: trying to do everything we can. By trying to change everything, we don't change anything, apart from generating stress for having spent a lot of effort without significant results.

Thinking clearly gives us the confidence to decide what to change in our reality to positively impact the system's totality rather than just isolated aspects, which would result in temporary results. We can visualize a future reality by becoming aware of the root cause.

By obtaining this understanding, we validate our purpose that drives a more fulfilling life. Therefore, we are ready to draw up a consistent outreach plan, allowing us to act with focus

Why act with focus?

Executing is making the plan alive. I would say it is at this stage that the process of living with purpose begins. At this stage, we give meaning to our daily routines. Many pursue life's meaning, which is about making daily meaningful and conscious choices.

Focus is crucial for the success of this significant day-to-day. Some behavioral profiles naturally exert focus as they envision a clear purpose. Others, despite having a purpose, tend to be more vulnerable to everyday distractions and complications.

Because of this, collaboration among the people involved is crucial. People must be aligned with common goals, which clarifies what to stop doing to achieve the goal. This is decisive and addresses the failure or success of a plan.

The following chapters present the six phases of this process as an invitation to embark on a journey of your own.

CHAPTER III – FULL CONSCIOUSNESS

Full consciousness is the ability to understand, become aware of our inner world, and perceive the reality around us in a way that allows us to act in alignment with our purposes and values rather than just following our instincts and reacting to circumstances (an inspired concept in the book Conscious Business by Fred Kofman).

As individuals, we have our inner system: our feelings, desires, ambitions, values, and behavioral tendencies. This way, we interact with the external system full of stimuli, information, and culture that condition our intuition and impulses. We have two options: live just reacting to this powerful external influence or develop autonomy to influence the circumstances and reality we want through our powerful inner system.

We can develop our consciousness through self-knowledge and live according to a purpose aligned with our needs and values. Therefore, we can be more intentional about the outcomes of reality.

Thinking clearly involves, above all else, being aware of our potential, values, and purposes to understand how we can positively influence reality.

The MVS method begins by developing full consciousness. Examining our internal system reveals what matters most to us and the values we cherish. We recognize the stories we have lived and taken pride in and how we have handled challenges, which shapes our profiles.

Our potential takes shape, and we better understand our behavioral tendencies, ways of thinking, and decision-making processes. We are no longer at the mercy of the circumstances and demands of the outside world. As we acquire full consciousness, we master our thoughts, emotions, and actions, positively impacting reality. This process awakens the best ambitions and a sense of purpose in life.

We are unique and have the inherent capacity to recognize, rethink, and recreate our reality.

In summary, we can achieve full consciousness by analyzing ourselves and our reality. This begins with recognizing our life story, identifying our core values, understanding our personal profile, and defining the purpose that drives us.

Acknowledging the life story

Acknowledging our life stories makes our values clear through the choices and challenges we have assumed during our journey. All struggles, challenges, and achievements reveal our inherent ability to be resilient. How we interact with people and situations defines our profile.

Knowing ourselves helps us make compatible choices in our personal and professional lives and boosts our willingness to improve and grow.

As the third pillar says, we must remember that people are good. Wrong assumptions lead to mistakes. Therefore, we must be disposed to review the situations we face. Without guilt, we must identify which assumption prevented us from succeeding and assume the learning point.

Recognizing our story is an exercise that should be practiced regularly. It is also a way of developing a sense of gratitude. In the United States, people often reflect their life stories on Thanksgiving Day, giving thanks for the year's outcomes and achievements. Universally, some people make it a habit to reflect on their lives and make new decisions. The traditional New Year's resolutions bring people hope for better days.

But what I propose is to write down the conquests and breakthroughs. Next to each event, note specifically what we excelled at or contributed at that moment. What characteristic did prevail in each achievement or challenge faced? On the other hand, we also recognize goals that were not achieved and what in us prevented them from happening. This exercise helps:

a. Increasing awareness of our potential.

b. Awake new opportunities.

c. Reinforce purpose awareness.

Reviewing the trajectory stirs motivation to refine our life purpose and reinvent the present. Therefore, self-knowledge begins by examining our lived story, achievements, and meaningful life episodes. That's how we realize our strengths. We start to be aware that there is a reason for everything. We add meaning to life and comprehend the stages of our evolutionary process. Our challenges present opportunities to demonstrate our strengths and foster learning and growth.

To be grateful!

By acknowledging facts, critical issues, and individuals for whom we are grateful, we shift from a state of need (what we lack) to a state of abundance (what we possess). This state of mind can awaken our potential and willingness to keep growing.

That is why it is essential to review our past. By doing so, we understand that, in one way or another, we are responsible for everything we have and observe around us. We are, for example, responsible for maintaining our mental and physical health, which can impact and influence what we reap from our reality, relationships, or professional performance.

How about starting to exercise gratitude by recognizing the person we have become?

Comparing ourselves to others is illogical because each individual has a unique life trajectory. The only worthwhile comparisons are those between our past and our present. An ascending curve can be envisioned.

Our choices, interactions with others, and responses to them shape our reality. We must also acknowledge the people we have had the privilege to meet. The gifts and blessings they offered us were not given by chance. This exercise rewires our thoughts, choices, habits, and decisions.

The practice of gratitude enhances the feeling of abundance, acknowledging our life stories. With this awareness, we can aspire to more significant dreams and develop stronger beliefs, fostering our capacity to adapt and grow.

Acknowledgments list benefits:

a. It decreases anxiety and stress, nurturing positive thoughts.

b. Improves self-esteem as we understand our value.

c. Awakes to the state of abundance (what I have) and rejects the state of scarcity (what I lack)

d. It enhances our readiness to face adversity by strengthening our state of mind. It facilitates our resilience and the ability to react positively in the face of adversity and obstacles.

With this mindset, we will be better prepared to continue our story by making more conscious choices and promoting who we are, our values, and our personal goals.

Forgiveness

We will be more prepared to forgive when we assume a state of gratitude. When we forgive, we release negative attachments and reinforce our welfare state.

In the book Authentic Happiness, written by the renowned propagator of Positive Psychology, Martin Seligman, he states:

"Insufficient appreciation of the good events in your past and overemphasizing the bad ones are the two culprits that undermine serenity, contentment, and satisfaction. There are two ways to bring these feelings about the past into contentment and satisfaction. Gratitude amplifies the relishing and appreciation of the good events, and rewriting the story by forgiveness loosens the power of the bad event to embitter (and actually can transform bad memories into good ones)." (book Authentic Happiness – 2020 edition - pages 88 and 89).

Martin Seligman mentions the intention to forgive as a prerequisite when reviewing the past. And Dr. Goldratt suggests choosing to believe that people are good.

By forgiving people, we are choosing to believe that they are good. Maybe they didn't get the chance to have their assumptions questioned so that they could have changed in time without harming anyone.

The same applies to us: 'We are good people,' and everything wrong we have done was based on assumptions we did not have the chance to reflect on and understand the basic cause-and-effect logic behind. What reality did we cause? Knowing what this means, we can free ourselves from guilt and take charge of our growth.

To follow values

Our life story helps us consciously identify which values drive our choices and decisions. Values are basic forms of conduct that shape our behavior.

Therefore, we can review areas of life, identify what values matter the most, and take them as principles that generate self-satisfaction. By doing this, we can quickly identify situations in which we exercise values that do not serve us. Looking at the past, we can detect when we were driven by greed or altruism, for example. Or when we were moved by pessimism or faith, pride or humility, indifference or empathy, falsehood or authenticity. When we are self-aware, it can promote growth and transformation. When we are unaware of the values that harm us, we continue to do the same and obtain the same results that do not satisfy us.

Values are not always positive. Some values guide people's conduct that distort their truth and integrity. Reviewing our behavior and recognizing which values favor or limit us from achieving success and fulfillment takes courage.

Positive values we recognize in our choices and attitudes make us feel fulfilled. Values should promote our self-esteem and make us proud of who we are. These values guide a person's legacy.

Freedom is fully living our values, regardless of the conditions and circumstances that life presents us.

Knowing our values makes us more likely to choose how to respond to situations rather than just reacting to them. In this way, we develop autonomy over what happens to us. We build our power to influence any challenge that life presents us positively.

What terms name these values that drive a person, a family, an institution, a company, or a community?

What values guide you at home with your family, at work, or running your business and your teams?

What values need to be respected so that you can continue to generate and reap results that positively impact your reality?

Figure 9 – Values

What values guide you? Which ones do you see in your daily actions or guide your personal and professional choices and decisions?

Be aware of these answers!

Self-confidence is shaped by recognizing and mastering the values that guide our success and personal and professional fulfillment.

The same is true for organizations. The more precise the values of a group with common purposes, the greater the engagement and differential in the market. The market perceives values that can promote a competitive edge.

It has never been more necessary to add value to products and services through the treatment and attitude we adopt when dealing with our customers, suppliers, partners, and employees. Technology and knowledge are easily accessible to everyone, but practicing clear values provides any system with success and continued growth.

Recognize the behavioral profile

Learning more about behavioral tendencies contributes to decision-making regarding choosing professional roles and elucidates those aspects limiting our growth or achievements.

Successful relationships require empathy, motivation, and persuasion. However, people differ in how they react to situations and in expectations. Each individual shares a particular contribution to a group, whether it is a family, a society, or an organization, to get the most out of its performance.

We need profiles that complement and support each other. Therefore, we do not expect everyone to respond to reality similarly. People differ in their thinking and actions.

Several services generate behavioral analysis assessments. The DISC model, well-known in the corporate environment, refers to four dimensions of human behavior: dominance, influence, stability, and compliance.

The DISC model was initially presented in 1928 when Dr. Marston published the book "Emotions of Normal People." This title implies that emotions matter and play a role in behavioral styles.

Behavior dimensions

Each person reacts differently to both favorable and unfavorable situations. For example, some are active in risky situations while others are more preventable. Some prefer stability and the certainty of the future, while others favor unpredictability and sudden changes in course.

Some feel comfortable in new social events. Others find it more challenging to approach them the first time and usually feel more comfortable until they develop a stronger bond. Others prefer to follow operational standards established by the environment. Others excel at acting according to their standards. Some still prioritize results, while others prioritize harmonious relationships.

The figure below demonstrates some profile traits in each of the four dimensions of behavior. These dimensions present themselves in different combinations and intensities from person to person.

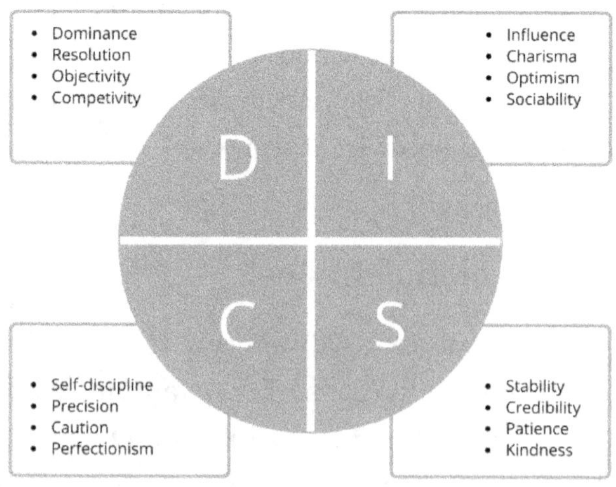

Figure 10 - Behavioral Profile

The reports and graphs demonstrate variations in three scenarios: self-image, work behavior, and behavior under pressure.

A trained professional must always conduct the feedback and obtain a written report. The feedback validates the profile analysis, recognizing facts and behaviors that prove its integrity. People are allowed to validate their behavior and identify favorable behavior tendencies in the current situation, as well as those that limit them from achieving more than they want in their personal and professional lives.

The most exciting aspect is that as we become familiar with our own behaviors, we start to recognize the behaviors of others with whom we interact. We realize this by observing their gestures, expressions, actions, reactions, preferences, and communication and leadership styles.

Although we are not static beings. The situations we live in and the challenges we face can possibly change the intensity of some behavioral dimensions over time.

For example, people with a high tendency to avoid conflict may learn to face and deal with it more naturally over time. In other cases, people with a low pace of decision-making under pressure can adapt based on their experiences and learn to make them more confident.

As we expose ourselves to life's inherent challenges, we may adapt and develop other behaviors naturally.

Some people are more resistant to change than others. This fact can facilitate or limit success in achieving their goals. One more reason to become aware of personal profiles is to adopt a mindset of confidence regarding our evolution and personal growth.

Once we know the characteristics and tendencies that shape our profile, it becomes possible to identify which ones limit us, allowing us to seek development and transform our behavior.

I had the opportunity to interact with psychologist Dr. Efrat Goldratt, also Dr. Goldratt's daughter, when she introduced her study about Enneagram. She presented the core dilemmas inherent to each kind of profile.

Understanding what holds us back and what is essential for our personal growth is not about changing who we are but rather about learning to recognize our behavioral tendencies and identifying win-win solutions.

As we already know, the cause-and-effect logic governs the results we obtain. Our behavioral mode operates on this principle as well. There must be a reason that motivates the willingness to go through the experience of transforming some behavior in everyday life, whether in a family, personal, or professional environment.

The coaching processes involve developing behavioral competencies. The TOC thinking processes greatly contribute to identifying the right competence that will promote significant improvement.

When we become aware of the right competence, we have an opportunity to apply some technique of development. One suggestion is to explore the meaning of competence, its universal characteristics, and who we know who successfully exercises this competence, for example. We can look at our past and remember when we experienced this behavior and how this happened. After reviewing, the next step is adapting to the current context and organizing the sequence of attitudes and tactics to put into practice.

Developing competence must be directly related to a practical objective and it becomes part of a plan.

At this point, we have advanced to a state of consciousness sufficient to realize the long-awaited purpose.

To have a purpose

The denotative sense of the word purpose is an objective, intent, or intention. Thus, individuals with purpose lead a life centered around a goal that enables them to achieve outcomes within their control.

There are no standardized guidelines for defining a purpose. The nature of a purpose can vary significantly from person to person. Or from organization to organization. Some people define purpose as something that brings them immense pleasure in life. Some define purpose as something that solves a big problem in their life. Some dedicate their lives to solving a significant problem for others. Some devote their purpose to a cause or passion.

Aware of our stories, behavioral profiles, and values, we are better prepared to clarify what we want from our lives from now on, adding more value to our existence.

Defining a consistent purpose constitutes the North Star that drives our decisions and gives meaning to our lives. It allows us to build meaningful lives.

At some point in life, people realize they need to rewire awareness of who they are to align with what they want. Seeking and assigning meaning to life is more productive than randomly looking for happiness.

There are many studies on happiness. Everyone wants to be happy. Even if not consciously, we automatically seek what makes us happy. In everyday life, moments bring comfort and satisfaction, which begin and finish without consistency.

Adversities intersperse these moments, and we try to reverse them, often fighting for our causes, tolerating, giving in, or giving up on situations and people.

Suddenly, we change cities, houses, jobs, partners, and employees. If this is done without full awareness of purpose, it only causes disharmony and instability while inhibiting growth without ensuring change for the better.

Why does pursuing happiness sometimes cause us frustration in such a competitive and challenging world? It seems that we never reached the point of arrival. When we arrive, the world and perspectives are already different.

We ceaselessly seek to improve our state of personal satisfaction. Becoming aware of our inner world and defining a goal has never been more suitable. A well-thought-out and truly lived purpose makes this search more effective and its achievement more lasting.

We are not where we are by chance. Within each of us lies a significant reason and the cherished opportunity to choose.

Do we seek a life geared toward survival, conformity, or meaningfulness?

The third option is usually preferred when I pose this comparative question during my workshops and coaching processes. It is remarkable how individuals desire to elevate their motivation and define what is meaningful. It requires a willingness to explore our potential and discover what holds us back. The good news is that there is a simple process for this discovery.

Dr. Goldratt used to ask:

"Do you want an easy life or a meaningful life?"

Meaningful living requires a thinking process, which leads us to obtain clarity and act with focus. Only after undergoing self-knowledge, it becomes possible to answer the following questions:

- How engaged, energized, and complete are you with life? What remains to be done?

- What can you do (what is under your control) to improve your reality?

- What is the reason why you do what you do today?

- How would you describe your reason for living?

- Do you have any dreams left in the past?

- What is your greatest ambition, or what do you desire to achieve?

- What do you think you know how to do well and could help others?

- What would you like to learn or master?

- What goals do you have in life that you would like to achieve?

If your answers come quickly and are satisfying, you already know your purpose or even live it! But you can clarify it, refine it, and understand what it brings to your life and those you care.

- How do you contribute to your reality by being who you are or doing what you do? Does that excite you?

When we discover a cause that motivates us and provides value, it signifies a purpose to pursue.

Save your answers and follow the process. There is more to explore that can help refine your purpose. It is usually challenging to verbalize immediately on the first attempt. It is necessary to express, register, and improve. What matters is that it must make absolute sense to you.

Therefore, the time has come to understand reality and its simplicity. Understand what prevents you from living more of your purpose. In this way, we will identify what to improve while making it possible to visualize what to change. It will give you the impetus to determine how to cause change. What impact does your purpose have on reality?

The purpose will be a fundamental part of the next stages of MVS, which will be covered in the following chapters.

Get involved, get excited about yourself, and believe you can live a full life!

Meaningful Life and Conscious Purpose go hand in hand.

In each challenge we face, there is a learning that will serve your growth and those around you.

Even when we express our biggest longings, desires, or goals and try to decipher what they mean, we will face challenges and have opportunities to learn and grow. It is the meaning, the noblest meaning, that human beings can allow themselves to live.

The same can be applied to leadership and companies. The more aware teams are about the company's purpose, the more aware they feel about their personal impact, developing a sense of belonging.

Successful leaders guide people by clearly communicating purposes and providing an environment where individuals manifest this alignment and trust in each other, thereby increasing their long-term commitment.

A meaningful purpose and self-awareness impact the harmony and growth of any system.

CHAPTER IV – INHERENT SIMPLICITY

Inherent Simplicity is the Pillar that supports the second phase of the process, during which we examine our current reality and clearly understand how it functions.

Cause and effect

As we have already discussed, every system is simple in its operation, no matter how complex it may initially seem. We must be willing to look at reality, understand the cause-and-effect relationships of the elements that compose it, and identify the root cause responsible for the performance.

The system can be an individual's personal or professional life. An ecosystem, a company, an institution, a family, a project, a community, a city, a state, a country, and its governments are considered equally complex systems. A few causes govern each system and are responsible for maintaining harmony.

In this chapter, we will review what makes an effective solution. An effective solution must be simple yet comprehensive in impact.

Imagine a complex situation in your personal or professional environment. When it is not in harmony, we can have multiple undesirable effects. What would be more effective? Are you trying to create isolated solutions for each of the effects? Or finding a single simple solution that triggers the reversal of these undesirable effects simultaneously?

According to the conventional approach, many elements in the same system indicate complexity. In the scientific approach, the more interconnected elements in a system, the simpler it is.

Therefore, the conventional approach seeks sophisticated solutions to solve a complex system, trying to change everything that can be improved. On the other hand, the scientific approach assumes that the more complex a system is, the simpler the solution must be, as it must touch only one element: the root cause.

This way of thinking helps us break the paradigm that solving a situation is very difficult or even impossible because it is too complex. Also, we know that sophisticated solutions don't work.

Often, the tendency to seek immediate solutions for each effect prevents us from seeing clearly. What is needed is identifying the unique and compelling root cause. It is like looking for a medicine for every patient's symptom without identifying the underlying disease causing most of the symptoms. There will be no cure.

Accurate root cause analysis lets us keep focus and cut distractions more naturally. When everyone is aware of the focus on improvement, communication tends to improve. Everyone understands they must subordinate other decisions to the preliminary goal to impact the system positively.

Conversely, when we attempt to implement multiple improvement actions simultaneously, we often lose sight of substantial results. Consequently, despite stressful efforts, this leads to poor outcomes.

The Wheel of Life

What change can you make in your personal life to achieve significant improvement?

The individual's reality is multi-faceted. The Wheel of Life is a tool created by the American Paul Meyer in 1960, adopted in self-knowledge processes, and used to detect the level of satisfaction in each area of life. Giving each area a score from 1 to 10 and connecting the dots, we usually see that the wheel is no longer circular, symbolizing how we feel as if our life is not "running" with stability.

But what should be improved and changed first?

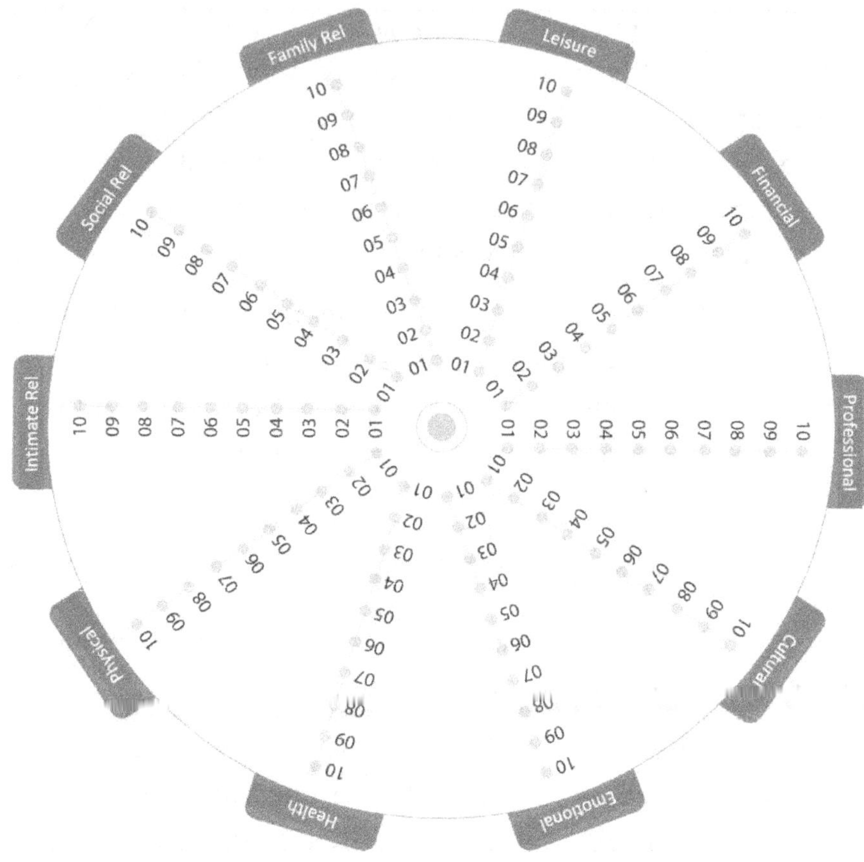

Figure 11 - The Wheel of Life

At this moment, TOC incisively contributes with its inherent simplicity concept. Checking the level of satisfaction and trying to improve everything that can be improved will not be productive. Understanding what effects prevent the satisfaction level in each living area from performing better becomes necessary. These effects come from asking the question: What is missing for 10?

We need to understand the interconnection between these effects. Connecting them in a cause-and-effect relationship leads to a root cause responsible for most of the effects.

Imagine this situation that initially seems complex. What if we created actions and attitudes for each undesirable effect we desire to improve?

- Emotional Area - I don't feel motivated at work and in my personal life.

- Relationship Area – I am under a lot of friction, complex connections, and lack of patience.

- Professional Area – I have excessive demands and feel unproductive.

- Health Area – I feel tired, heart problems, depression, high levels of cortisol, and insomnia.

- Leisure/Social Area – I don't feel like going on social activities.

- Family Area – I don't feel like a good parent; scattered children; lack of family unity.

The question would be:

What problem are we trying to solve? What "disease" causes these symptoms? Is it impaired function, behavioral tendencies that inhibit productivity, a lack of a plan, or simply a lack of healthy habits?

But if that person connected these elements in a cause-and-effect relationship and explored the logic that sustains this reality, he would undoubtedly arrive at a single cause responsible for all other undesirable effects. Understanding the root cause and discovering the dilemma that prevents its reversal is how to find the ultimate solution.

The phrases above identify the "undesirable effects" in each area of life. They are verbalized in a way that holds us accountable and does not blame someone else. These are current facts, not speculated causes. There have been attempts to solve them with no success. Analyzing the system makes it possible to identify which effect to change first in a way that significantly impacts others.

Let's say the person started with physical health. Enhancing physical performance would improve self-esteem. Cortisol levels would decrease, and energy levels would rise, leading to better focus at work. Consequently, with an improved mood, this person would regain patience in his personal and workplace relationships, enhancing social harmony and disposition.

It is a simplified example, but no less important in finding a solution. The same principle of inherent simplicity can be used to address both common and atypical situations.

What would prevent this individual from improving his physical health? He has keen intuition, and why didn't he act sooner? Could it be the existence of an inner dilemma?

The solution and the thinking process will be presented below to unravel a system's inherent simplicity in the personal and professional scope.

Current Reality Tree – CRT

The current Reality Tree is a tool that organizes the elements that build the reality of a person, a family, or an organizational system. The technique connects these elements using the principle of cause and effect.

When reality is disharmony, this tool helps us locate the few elements, if not the only factor, responsible for generating all the other undesirable effects.

Next, I present a case based on a client's reality already in the phase – Inherent Simplicity.

Having already achieved self-awareness, this large family business executive director found himself in a personal and professional context that was at odds with his fundamental values and life purpose. As the eldest of the five brothers, he had assumed the company director role for about a year, having already worked in several areas for fifteen years. His father was the president of the company.

There were undesirable effects that eroded daily operations and the significance of everything, affecting harmony both within the company and in family life, as follows:

- My mental energy is low.

- I feel insecure about my leadership skills.

- I feel unproductive.

- My physical health is impaired.

- I have a lot of work piling up.

- I deliver poor attention to important projects.

- I am overwhelmed with the demands of my teams.

- The results are invisible.

- There are a lot of discussions with the president.

- I do not have time available for my family.

The verbalization of these effects was refined to more accurately represent the reality of the facts. For example, feeling demanded differs from being required. The client realized that people did not demand from him, but he was the one who felt that way, and something was preventing him from reversing it.

However, a relevant purpose has been previously defined, and this CEO has been encouraged to face his reality and devise a solution and execution plan to reverse it into a more meaningful and desirable one.

Utilizing the cause-and-effect logic process, the following Current Reality Tree was developed:

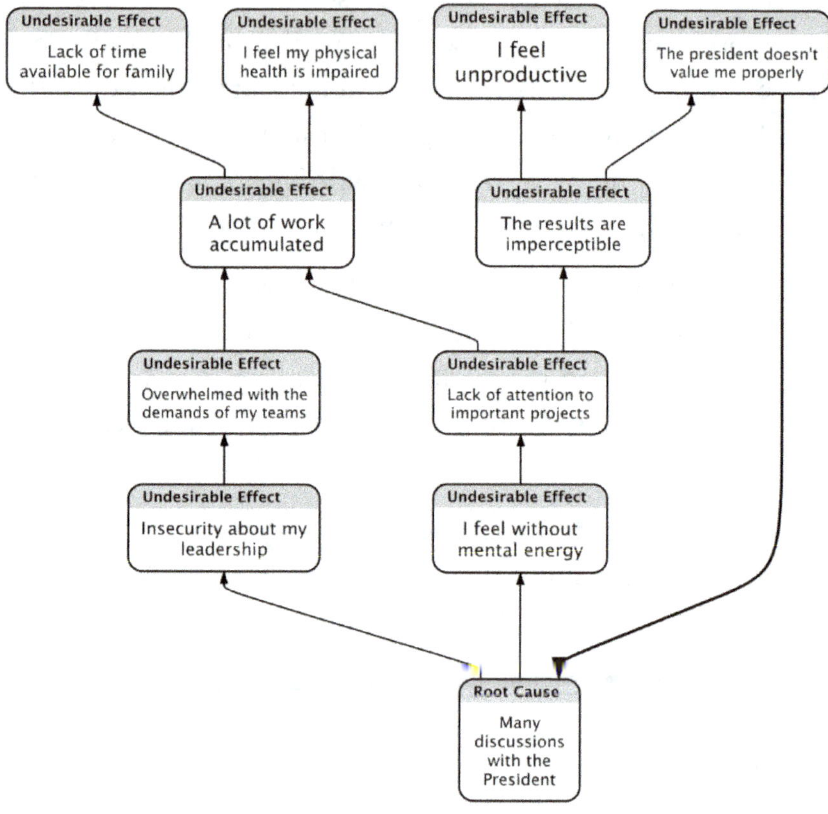

Figure 12 - Current Reality Tree

When the executive connected the undesirable effects in a cause-and-effect relationship, he quickly realized that there was only one point he had to address and turn around to positively impact all the other effects: many arguments with his father, the company's president. This factor was the root cause that drained his energy and generated insecurity about his leadership skills. Many of these arguments would often occur in front of other directors and teams.

To compensate for his insecurity in leadership, the executive tried to be always available to meet his team's demands. Here, it is worth noting that top management's lack of alignment and harmony generates an insecure team environment.

Therefore, his attempts to prove himself as a good leader by "putting out fires" prevented him from focusing on more critical projects that would strengthen the company.

This factor generated adverse effects regarding satisfactory professional and personal results. His backlog of work increased in the executive routine, affecting his personal life. Health and family time were equally impacted, while the most significant pain rummaged through his sleep: the feeling of not being professionally recognized by his father.

Building the Current Reality Tree (fig.12) was a critical exercise that revealed the inherent simplicity of this executive's context. Each effect was worked on to find the most accurate and actual verbalization. The connection between these effects brought clarity and allowed him to find the right focus to overcome.

But what was preventing him from reversing these exhausting discussions in alignment? A dilemma was unraveled, and the solution to this dilemma would be the answer. The direction of his solution will be presented in the next chapter.

Identifying dilemmas and root causes that prevent a professional from performing satisfactorily is the raw material for unlocking inherent potential. There certainly was a solution to this dilemma, which came through challenging assumptions supporting it.

Valid needs are usually connected to contradictory or exclusionary actions that prevent this potential from performing at its best. After challenging the assumptions outlined in the previous diagram, a solution, referred to as the injection, was identified. This "treatment" eliminated the problem.

Often, individuals spend years and decades attempting to manage each undesirable symptom, either fighting tirelessly or resigning themselves to an unhappy life or succumbing to psychosomatic illnesses due to dissatisfaction with themselves or the circumstances.

Working on the causes of problems is a way to evoke transformation, overcoming, success, and health. Not to mention time, a resource that is only scarce when we waste management attention acting on what is unnecessary.

Nowadays, it is common for people to seek development in high performance precisely because they recognize there is no time for all the demands they submit. This search for high performance and results is never fully achieved when there is a lack of clarity about reality and self-knowledge.

When our actions, lifestyle, or thoughts are out of alignment with our values and purposes, we begin to observe detrimental effects on our physical and mental health.

Thus, while reality can be complex, there is an inherent simplicity in the way it works.

This represents the scientific approach to thinking about and perceiving reality. If we learn to perceive reality through the lens of cause and effect, we will see more clearly, make better decisions, and act with greater consciousness and effectiveness.

Searching for results is a prevalent practice in corporate environments. After two decades of dedication and experience, upon becoming a director, my client encountered a dilemma that hindered his optimal performance and full realization of his potential. What could this be? What was the single factor preventing him from maximizing his own potential and the potential of the company?

The following chapter will explore how we identify the barriers that prevent individuals from reaching more of their potential, having acknowledged the inherent simplicity of their own reality.

CHAPTER V – DIRECTION OF THE SOLUTION

The Cloud

As discussed in the previous chapter, the path of a solution typically begins with understanding and resolving a dilemma. The solution will unlock the system's inherent capability and elevate it to a higher level of performance than it currently has.

The solution often represents a paradigm shift. Some assumptions that we have not challenged before originating a solution for change. The dilemma, therefore, is considered the raw material that causes the ultimate solution.

Articulating the cloud and validating its logic is the initial step that confronts us with the dilemma.

Dr. Goldratt named this process 'evaporating the cloud.' He was inspired by the book Illusions by Richard Bach, in which the author uses this expression and, in an excerpt, says, "If you want to take a cloud out of your life, don't make a scene out of it; just relax and take it out of your thought. That's it."

Conflicts between two parties or internal personal dilemmas are natural parts of life, typically addressed through fighting, yielding, or ignoring. Some behavior profiles tend to yield to avoid conflict with others. Consequently, they avoid understanding the conflict and fail to solve it.

Avoiding conflict or dilemma leads us to sacrifice something essential and accept an unsatisfactory reality, believing we effectively address the problem. The cloud tool contributes significantly to providing solutions and recovering the harmony inherent to every reality.

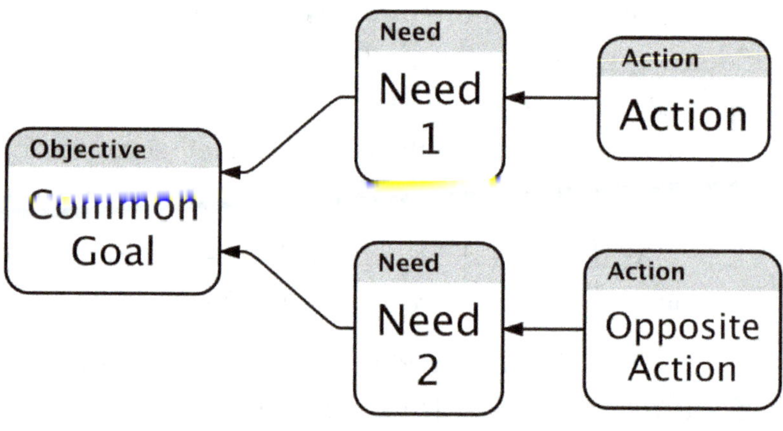

Figure 13 - The Cloud

The cloud is a diagram where we can spell out a problem related to any situation involving contradictory actions or desires between two sides with a common goal.

Dilemma

The cloud makes us realize the needs that underpin our actions. Satisfying these needs guarantees harmony on both sides of a dilemma. However, we often act on one of our needs but jeopardize another need that is also important to us.

TOC states that making the dilemma explicit and understanding the logic of the installed problem fosters finding solutions for improvement and achieving significant results in any situation. Removing dilemmas generates a direction for the solution and restores harmony.

A solution must account for both sides of the dilemma to be effective. The dilemma or conflict will remain when the solution solves only one side and leaves the other aside.

The conflict between two people

The cloud also allows two conflicting people to listen to each other first. Pay attention to the impact of our actions or desires on the needs of the other with whom we have a common goal.

There is no other way to achieve harmony between two people than to develop a willingness to understand each other's logic. And to be genuinely interested in the relationship's success to protect a common goal.

The most interesting thing is that when action is characterized by doing something wrong, there is still a need that initially led to that action. When challenging the validity of a need or the actions taken to satisfy it, solutions and paradigm shifts emerge that were not considered beforehand. At this point, it seems easier for us to understand that, by definition, people are good.

Evaporating the cloud technique

Let's go back to the cloud presented in the previous chapter about the CEO to understand how the 'evaporating the cloud technique' was applied.

After validating the thinking process and reading the CRT - Current Reality Tree- it became clear that a solution was necessary to avoid discussions that harm management attention, leadership, and the company's results. What triggered these discussions were contradictory needs and actions. The following cloud diagram presents how the dilemma was described in this case:

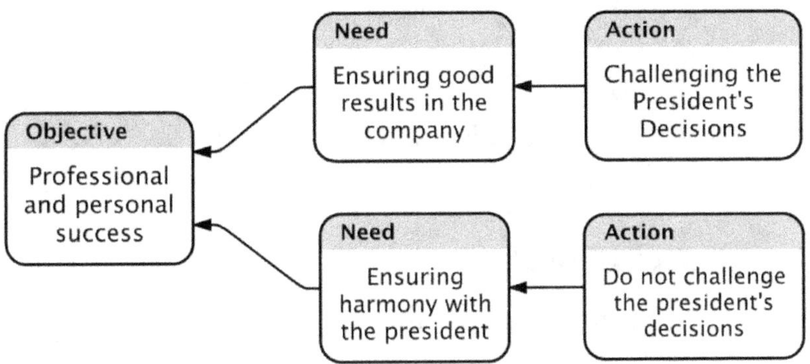

Figure 14 - Personal Success Cloud

Once the cloud is validated, the conflict is exposed. The conflict is the raw material used to find a win-win solution to eliminate the problem.

We need to challenge the assumptions that underpin the cloud. Explain the relationship of the five entities to each other.

Challenging our logic is a great opportunity to develop better solutions.

Objective:

A- Personal and professional success.

Valid Needs:

B- Ensure good results for the company.

C- Ensure harmony with the president.

Contradictory actions:

D- Challenge the president's decisions.

D'- Do not challenge the president's decision.

Cloud reading

To achieve personal success (A), on the one hand, I need to ensure good results in the company (B). And to ensure good results in the company, I need to challenge the president's decisions (D). But on the other hand, for personal success (A), I also need to ensure harmony with the president (C). And, to ensure harmony, I must not challenge his ideas (D').

After verifying the logic, it's time to ask questions. The answers will eventually lead to a wrong assumption, leading to a paradigm shift, evaporating the cloud. Otherwise, a new action possible appears to dismiss the dilemma.

Challenging the assumptions:

1. Challenging the B-D link:

Why do you need to challenge the president's decisions to guarantee good results in the company?

Is this the only way to guarantee the results?

2. Challenging the C-D'link:

On the other hand, why do you need to stop challenging the president to be in harmony with him?

Is stopping challenging the president's ideas the only way to ensure harmony?

3. Challenging the D-C link:

When does challenging the president's decisions threaten harmony?

4. Challenging the link D'-B:

When does not challenge the president's decisions threaten the company's bottom line?

5. Challenging D-D':

Why can't D and D' coexist?

Is there a third single action that eliminates this question of whether to challenge or not to challenge the president's ideas and guarantees good company results while maintaining harmony with the father/president?

It is an uncommon occurrence with no standard responses or a single solution. Another simple reasoning can be added to any of the answers originating from the questions above:

Unless.

This simple expression can extend thinking and promote innovative and disruptive ideas, especially in difficult or even impossible issues to solve, but if they weren't, it would change everything.

After discussing all the answers to the above questions in the session, the executive discovered the wrong assumption, the one that most made him available to challenge his potential. In the B-D connection, he found the injection that, when applied, could undo the cloud.

Challenging the B-D connection:

Why is the only way to challenge the president's decisions to guarantee good results in the company?

Answer: To grow and improve revenue, the company must innovate production and distribution processes to adapt to a new reality. The company's conservative founding president, who remains firm in the power of decisions, does not accept change in the processes. Decision meetings become endless discussions with no results.

It is difficult **unless** you can decouple the president's role and power in making the right strategic decisions from the director's control in execution. This development process was consolidated in four months through individual and joint coaching sessions with the president and director. Both reviewed their common objective and addressed family harmony and the company's continuous growth.

As a result, meetings began to be prepared with a focus on results, and decisions by the director began to be shared based on the president's objectives. That is, the content of what was discussed in meetings with the president and the format of these meetings brought greater objectivity and focus, avoiding wasting time with details and threats that resulted in discussions, also destabilizing the team of directors.

The director developed a productivity plan, always addressing the president's objectives and strategic vision.

Next, the cloud tool presents a win-win solution, covering both valid needs and the common objective. From then on, the dilemma no longer exists.

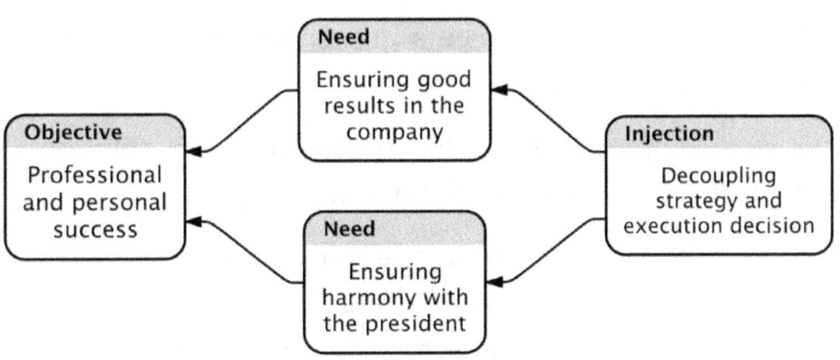

Figure 15 - The Injection

This simple yet robust attitude had far-reaching repercussions beyond the alignment between the president-father and the director-son. Still, it achieved an improvement in the performance levels of the company as a whole. Family harmony has been restored to a higher level. And the motivation to execute the productivity plan with confident and influential leadership took place in the direction of a common purpose.

Therefore, the way to evaporate the cloud is often to change the action to one that satisfies the core needs without creating threats. Actions can be changed or added, but needs must be validated and remain toward the common goal.

The important thing is that the focus on – what to change – provides significant personal and professional improvements and benefits for those involved.

At this moment, the direction of the solution emerges, which will define what to change.

The solution to the dilemma triggers – what to change, knowing that by generating the change, we will have a clear new reality – for what to change. We call this new reality the Future Reality Tree.

Future Reality Tree – FRT

Time to visualize the effects of the change in the future. There were undesirable effects that were connected to a root cause. A dilemma stood in the way of this root cause. What solved this dilemma was an injection.

If applied with an effective plan, this injection will reverse the undesirable effects and lead to achieving a full life, contemplating a more significant reason: the purpose defined previously.

Thinking clearly means being aware of obstacles and overcoming them through assertive actions. Visualizing the near future from our current stage will inspire us to transform any possible obstacle into intermediate objectives. Therefore, thinking clearly also includes anticipating what is evident. It is necessary to have an action plan to open the way and let the injection flow.

The Future Reality Tree is designed to check the injection's impact on reversing the undesirable effects of the current reality into desirable ones.

It is an extraordinary human tendency: whenever we are certain of our goals, we can confront any challenge to achieve them. For this reason, driven by enthusiasm, we often tend to jump into action too quickly without thinking about the consequences and obstacles of our decisions.

At this stage, it is necessary to foresee and prune possible negative branches arising from the change. The biggest problem that prevents the success of a change action, whether in personal or professional life, is not thinking systemically and trying to predict if other areas or people may be affected, harming the harmony in implementing the plan. There will always be an action that needs to be considered in advance. The principle of cause and effect makes this possible.

In the following pages, we present a model for developing a Future Reality Tree from an injection – namely, the solution that, once implemented, enhances the performance of both personal and professional contexts.

Subsequently, we started to build the Future Reality Tree—for what to change—to validate the injection's application and check its positive impact on most of the undesirable effects.

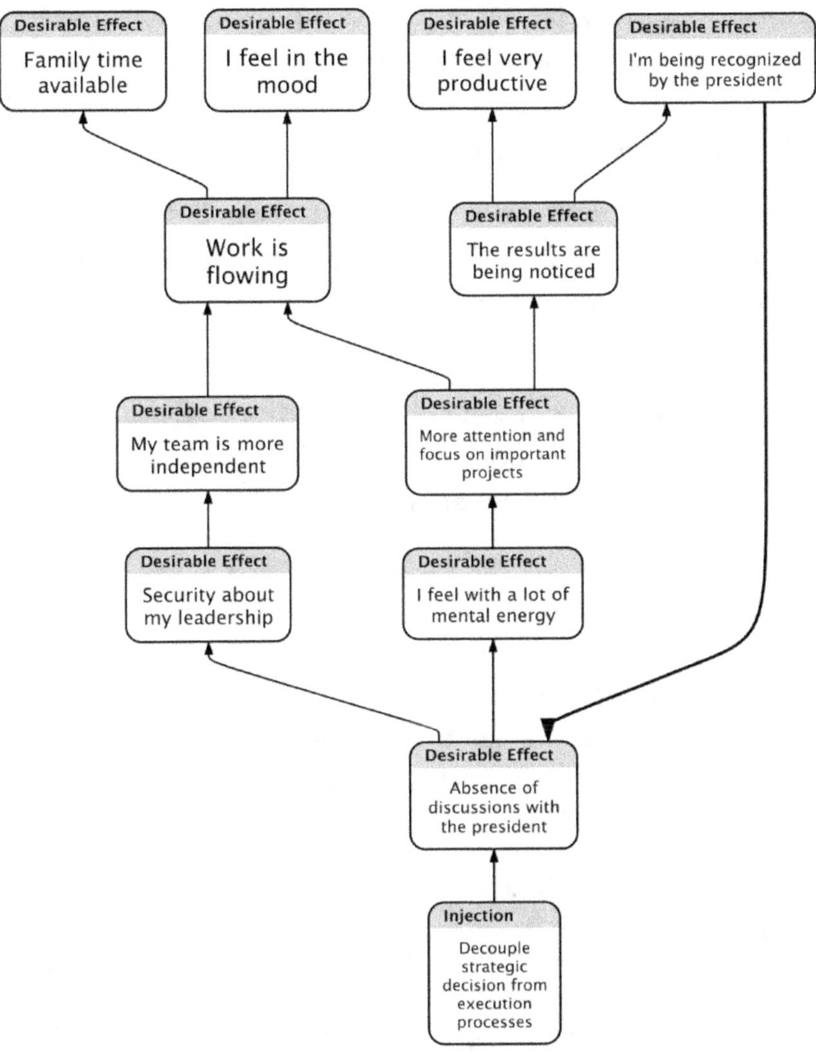

Figure 16 - Future Reality Tree

By finalizing the Future Reality Tree, we gained a clear vision of the desired reality, which embraced a sense of purpose and focus that had been missing from the beginning of the process.

Applying logic to unravel reality and solutions, whether in life or business, contributes to obtaining clarity, which improves our perspective enhancing our emotional state.

In addition, I have noticed that the TOC thinking processes alleviate stress by clarifying our focus and facilitating management attention.

Roadmap

With this systemic view and after deciphering what to change and what to change for, the future reality becomes visible, and it is now time to define how to cause the change.

We call this action plan the Meaningful Life Roadmap.

The roadmap is an opportunity to address the Future Reality Tree, organize actions, and overcome obstacles. Each validated obstacle is transformed into an intermediate objective. These objectives define organized actions sequentially: prerequisites and parallel actions.

Once we have this clarity, obstacles inherent in the process become new measures to guarantee the plan. When creating the roadmap, paying attention to obstacles ensures that it flows so that we can enjoy the journey and focus on what really matters.

Obstacles are all factors that can limit or prevent our goals from generating the expected results in an agile way. They can be physical, behavioral, or even emotional. Physical resources such as the lack of a suitable environment, agile technology, or even enough money need to be foreseen for us to generate means to solve them. If not foreseen and resolved in advance, behavioral trends, habits, the emotional state of people involved, and lack of collaboration can be impeditive factors.

In the case of the executive, three obstacles were identified for the implementation of the solution, such as decoupling the strategic decision of the president from the decisions of the execution process:

1. The company's senior staff habitually involved the president in day-to-day operations.

2. Meetings with the president were fraught with multitasking, which caused the coverage of many items to be disorganized and made it impossible to finalize the critical topics.

3. In a typical father-son dynamic, the executive had a powerful tendency to argue with the president, even when ensuring a different course was not essential.

Intermediate objectives and the respective actions to achieve these objectives were defined for each obstacle, as shown in the roadmap in Figure 16.

1. Train senior staff in the new work system to no longer involve the president.

2. Prepare a full kit for meetings to focus on important issues.

3. Develop positive communication skills to deal with the tendency to argue with the parent. This is covered more in-depth in another phase of the MVS method: Effective Interaction.

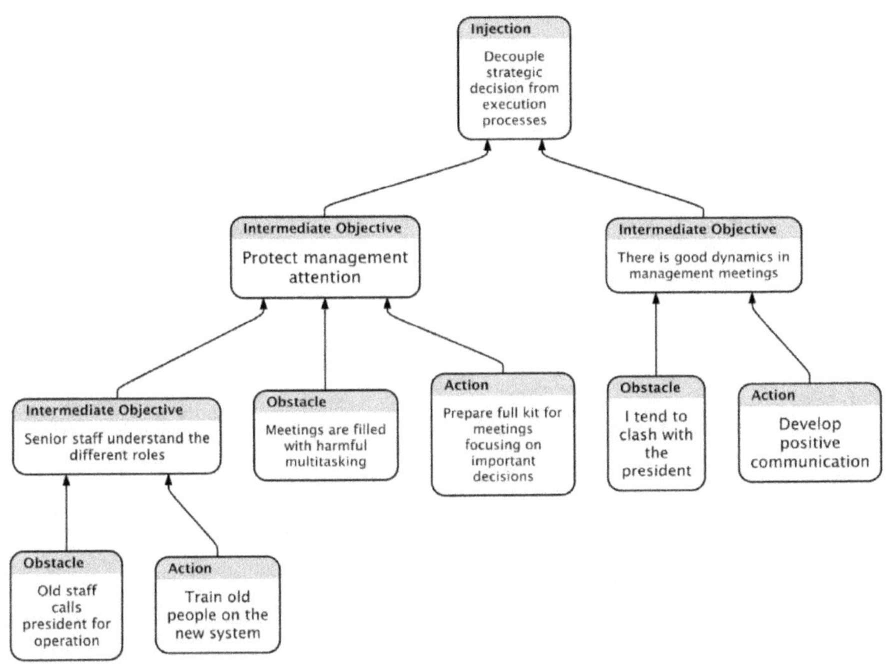

Fig.17 - Roadmap

Defining a roadmap will keep us going ahead while we can enjoy the journey. We may even be surprised to achieve the benefits before our deadline. This feeling of having conquered time makes us feel accomplished and productive. We take control of our daily lives and create conditions for everything to happen successfully. This self-confidence drives us to continue creating, building, and growing.

The roadmap is designed to accomplish a greater purpose.

Focus principle

"Management attention is the ultimate constraint."

Dr. Eliyahu Goldratt

Where we place our attention most of the time is the factor that will either leverage or obstruct the flow of the process. It is important to subordinate all decisions that arise along the way to decisions that guarantee the achievement of the primary goal. When we know our goals, we cannot let other distractions interfere and move us away from what has been decided. The focus prevents us from easily falling into the trap of shifting our attention elsewhere.

If some new possibility arises, we have a question:

Does this opportunity bring me closer, make it easier, or push me away from the primary goal?

Any decision that diverts us from the goal or damage it must be avoided. That's why maintaining consistent follow-up is crucial to validate the course.

Any decision or action that is supposed to be productive but doesn't bring me closer to my goal is ineffective.

Focus involves a complete and efficient awareness of what to do and what to stop doing, facilitating the flow.

With this focus in mind, we initiate the execution stage:

Act with focus, which entails how to cause change.

At this stage, we revisit the behavioral analysis delivered at the start of the process and apply it in practice. This is regarding our daily attitudes and actions, as we are all susceptible to external disturbances and prone to the internal pitfalls inherent to human nature.

Considering these critical aspects, let's align our awareness with a noble and ambitious goal in our lives.

We must ensure a path we are proud of, one where the stars are always visible and all the clouds can evaporate.

Cut out distractions

Similarly, realities about modern life, which are replete with new opportunities, also capture our attention. We must be vigilant about potential disruptions to our workflow, which often emerge subtly and may not initially seem to threaten our focus.

Of course, mid-execution readjustments can be crucial if they favor achieving our goals. External changes may also occur; we must be attuned to the necessary adaptations. However, with a clear direction and understanding of our goals, it becomes easier to identify distractions.

We are constantly making decisions. Therefore, to decide means to eliminate other possibilities. The Latin origin of 'decide' connotes cutting: de (off) and 'caedere' (to cut).

As I write this book, many worldwide suffer the consequences of a pandemic that has significantly impacted health and the economy. Many have had to reinvent themselves to survive. Others, lacking clear purposes and plans, felt the need to create them. For the same reasons, some abandoned their businesses, failing to recognize timely opportunities for change. However, those who maintained the habit of not succumbing to distractions possessed greater resilience to confront a crisis like the one caused by the virus.

Especially at work, we are frequently exposed to noise, interruptions, side conversations, unsolicited messages, and emails that clutter our inboxes. Protecting our attention and work environment improves our concentration flow, optimizing time in favor of our goals and our plans. We will accomplish more in less time, making us feel productive rather than captive to circumstances.

Therefore, a clear and robust purpose-oriented plan safeguards our daily lives, enhances our productivity through actions that really matter, and will make a difference in our personal and professional lives.

Avoid Multitasking

Starting many tasks simultaneously may seem a way to optimize time when these tasks are not excluded, as can be the case with some types of projects. Different actions do not use the same resources and can occur entirely in parallel. An executive woman may start the washing machine work and bake a cake while making a work call.

On the other hand, it would be impossible to be effective if she collected the clothes, stopped mixing the cake ingredients, and interrupted the task of paying attention to her son, who asked for help with schoolwork. When she returned to the cake mix, a call made her answer and handled an Excel spreadsheet.

When the executive woman returned to the cake, she would no longer remember if she had already added half a spoon of salt, and when she went to the laundry, she would not be sure if she had already added the softener. At the same time, the Excel spreadsheet would wait to be finished. This person, a simple and typical example of executives and mothers at the home office, helps us understand when multitasking is harmful.

Studies show that it is not always possible to fully focus on multiple projects simultaneously. Every time our focus is interrupted, we lose quality and margin of success performance. We can even perform several tasks alternately but lose time and quality.

Many tools and task management features make people more productive and lessen the harmful effects of multitasking. However, there are other concepts to explore first.

Guarantee Full Kit

How often do we encounter something extremely important to accomplish with high expectations for results? After starting the execution, do we lack any key ingredients to accomplish the task?

Often, the urge to achieve results, whether in domestic contexts, personal life, on a dream trip, in a simple recipe, at an important dinner, or in a business meeting, leads people to not invest time in preparation before starting execution. To be productive, we rush steps that make us stop later to solve when it's not too late.

The full kit concept is part of the TOC approach and means checking and gathering everything needed to complete a task or project before starting execution. Investing time before provides time gain, guaranteeing quality and success in the results. In the words of Kristen Cox, former executive director of the Utah government and TOC expert:

"Sometimes we need to go slower to get faster."

Therefore, organizing the full kit is part of the preparation. Investing time gathering the correct information, documents, approvals, tools, and other particular requirements of each type of activity or project before executing will avoid postponements, rework, waste of time, and multitasking, if not wasting valuable opportunities. As famously quoted by Seneca:

"Luck is what happens when preparation meets opportunity."

Dr. Eli Goldratt added:

"Bad luck is when lack of preparation meets reality."

In an article, Rami Goldratt highlights preparedness as 'an essential professional's attribute'.

When a culture of preparation is practiced throughout an organization, employee and process performance improves significantly.

One of the most frequent complaints I hear from executives is about unproductive or interminable meetings, precisely because of the lack of a full kit. Either there was a lack of information, incorrect information was provided, the participants were not properly updated, or they were unaware of the issues at hand, leaving them unprepared. Discussions start before all the implications, required resources, and accurate numbers are known, making delays in decision-making natural.

In the context of prospecting meetings, collecting information about the company and the contact is an essential part of the preparation before meeting the prospect for the first time. Understanding the context of the potential client, their vision, and possible challenges is an essential component of the full kit and involves practicing empathy. It involves considering everything that might be important to have readily available. Preparing in advance can be a key differentiator in face-to-face interaction and advancing the prospect to the next stage of the sales process. Therefore, proper preparation can significantly influence the quality of the relationships, the prospect engagement, and the company's revenue.

The full kit should be considered essential in executing daily activities, both personal and professional. It ensures smooth operations and success in achieving desired outcomes while maintaining harmony and focus and preventing unnecessary stress, which are crucial for effective execution.

Define habits

Promoting effective execution also involves recognizing the essential habits that support our purposes and goals and identifying habits that may undermine them, often unconsciously and intuitively. It is common to adhere to habits that are detrimental to us and do not contribute to our physical and mental health. Conversely, we can adopt habits that enhance our performance.

For instance, maintaining good sleeping hygiene, consuming a nutrient-rich diet, engaging in regular physical activity, and practicing meditation can all improve our mental and physical states and make us more equipped and willing to handle daily challenges.

Therefore, they are habits that favor our mental and physical energy.

Some habits also significantly influence our emotional state and, thus, our thoughts and decisions. For example, listening to inspiring music, engaging with uplifting media, and choosing enriching reading material can stimulate positive brain frequencies, leading to new insights, ideas, and aspirations that influence our choices and guide us toward our desires.

Additionally, it is vital to cultivate habits that contribute to our development, enhance our mastery and expertise in relevant subjects, and make a practical impact on our journey.

We can relate this to a passion commonly observed among athletes, artists, musicians, and entrepreneurs. Nothing restrains or deviates them from their goals. When the purposes are clear and meaningful, they drive us to acquire good habits, which we practice consciously without much effort.

It is crucial to choose the main habits that enhance the effective execution of our plans and identify which ones to avoid. Saying no to detrimental habits becomes straightforward when we have compelling reasons for doing so. Resistance to developing new habits occurs when the positive benefits are unclear.

It is during the execution stage that life begins to have a deeper meaning, and each day starts to make more sense. We are conscious of the reality we are creating. The state of satisfaction and fulfillment within ourselves becomes evident. I am positive that this state is what makes us complete and happy.

Therefore, it is up to us to decide how we manage our attention. By recognizing this, we can adopt clear and straightforward attitudes that enhance our focus. Focus involves the ability to say no when necessary. Focus goes beyond knowing what to do. It is about knowing what not to do. This concept raises the level of productivity.

Agenda and productivity

With a developed conscience and a clear purpose, managing the daily schedule more effectively becomes possible.

More than just a tool for tracking appointments, the agenda becomes an instrument for managing our personal and professional successes. This is our weekly goal. Whether you're a housewife, a self-employed professional, an executive, a salesperson, or even a student, having a clear vision for the week can significantly enhance our sense of productivity.

Decisions must be made weekly. What do I aim to accomplish by Friday to bring me closer to or facilitate achieving my purpose?

It's time to meet weekly goals to raise the bar for next week's achievement. All the planning outlined in the previous roadmap must be analyzed to make the best decisions weekly, monthly, or annually. The objective is to reduce pressure and increase the flow towards the greater purpose.

We acquire a sense of focus that makes us aware of quantifying the time we should dedicate to a particular life goal. Where should I put most of my attention and dedication to grow my personal life, career, or company?

This is the first step in making decisions and understanding how we can capitalize on one of our most important resources: our time. We need to view time as a resource in our favor, not as a constraint.

Many people find it difficult to say no to others without losing kindness because they are unclear about their goals. Viewing our planner as a tool that organizes a list of achievements around meaningful goals makes our daily lives more enjoyable. It helps to protect our focus on what matters most and prevents us from becoming captive to external demands and distractions. Sometimes, saying no is an opportunity to help others organize themselves, not only in an executive environment but also, for example, in the specific leadership exercised between parents and children.

On the other hand, using an agenda with buffers is a concept widely applied in project management throughout the Theory of Constraints. If we have a clear idea of what is most important to accomplish in the agenda, it is possible to allow spaces of time in everyday life for potential sudden unpredicted issues that deserve our attention. Or even enable lengths of time to be used to replenish our mental or physical energy.

The key is to reach Friday, review our accomplished objectives, and feel satisfied with our productivity. It may have been a week filled with accomplishments, although with positive outcomes, making the natural stress experienced beneficial rather than harmful.

I often hear executives complaining about running out of time, making decisions in meetings, and feeling exhausted and frustrated because things didn't work out as expected. I often also hear the expression 'putting out fires' used by many who lack a clear vision of their scope and an awareness of purpose. Their schedules are at the mercy of constant interruptions and problems to solve, causing them to overlook a crucial leadership skill: effective delegation.

Many tools can contribute to achieving a productive agenda and be adopted as allies in everyday life. I particularly value the '1 Page Productivity Planner' I discovered while attending the High-Performance Academy led by the American coach, author, and speaker Brendon Burchard. It is readily available online.

The first part of the tool consists of a holistic view of the projects in our lives that are under our responsibility. It involves identifying the important projects corresponding to the most important life areas and giving them titles. Next, the tasks are listed under headlines, outlining what needs to be done for these projects to advance over time.

The second part consists of two lists: the people we must contact to advance the projects and those from whom we await updates.

The third part of the 1 Page focuses on our weekly planning. Now is the time to determine the agenda and prioritize from the overview of the first and second parts of the 1Page. What we need to ask ourselves:

How much time should I dedicate to each project? Which projects will most significantly impact my personal and professional goals? By being conscious of priorities, we can balance the time and attention to each project and schedule accordingly.

We need to make these decisions weekly to reclaim our sense of productivity. What we decide to do in one week will shape the flow of the following week.

Additionally, including some TOC concepts in this simple 1Page tool can significantly impact results.

The focus is to develop effective planning based on priorities considering the execution of the roadmap defined previously on how to cause the change for a meaningful life.

The tool presented is just a suggestion. Tools and technological resources are highly personal and should be tailored to meet the specific needs of each individual. What matters most is the agility of access.

Focusing on priorities allows us to determine which projects will occupy most of our time.

After progressing from defining a purpose (full consciousness) to the roadmap (direction of the solution), we will manage productivity and focus more effectively in our personal or professional lives.

Regarding productivity, especially in the professional environment, it is common for employees to create endless to-do lists in their eagerness to become productive professionals. These lists obscure the vision of results whether they do not plan focused on a pre-defined strategic purpose. However, when the purpose is defined, analyzing each item on the list from the perspective of significant impact drops to half or even a third of what was initially thought. Many items are delegated, placed as future goals, or even eliminated. Clarifying goals and refining focus promote enormous benefits for everyday life while strengthening the sense of meaning.

As mentioned before, according to the Theory of Constraints, the focus is not on doing everything that can be done but on what needs to be done. Our greater purpose determines what needs to be done.

From this angle comes the sense of priority, deciding where to put most of our attention. Thus, planning an agenda based on achievements, not just routine tasks without meaning, contributes to our fulfillment in life.

We consider success the weekly objectives achieved that bring us closer to our purposes, whether personal or related to the companies and institutions we work for.

It is essential to note that making weekly decisions and blocking time for meaningful tasks requires another principle that protects our management attention: a time buffer. An agenda where all appointments and tasks are hourly is ineffective. Contrary to what some might say, a full agenda is not effective.

Being busy from hour to hour is not a synonym for productivity. We need to allow time for it. A buffer between tasks is necessary to accommodate natural extension in time and new important demands that may arise.

It is recommended that important tasks be decided on and executed successfully and entirely during the week. This is more efficient than scheduling everything that can be done hourly, which often becomes impossible.

Having a scope focus under a more macro view with a robust plan that carries, in addition to a time buffer, a sense of purpose and priority will bring much more value to time as it becomes an ally and not a constraint

The full kit practice mentioned before also needs time to plan a successful agenda. The full kit collaborates with agility in terms of time and quality of results. Investing time in preparing everything needed can shorten its execution time and prevent multitasking. This preparation helps avoid interruptions in retrieving missing items during the task.

Additionally, it is worth noting that respect is established when we share and communicate our plans in a way that aligns with a common purpose. A senior executive client observed that a structured schedule not only enhances productivity for himself and his team but also teaches the importance of prioritizing. Once we learn to focus on what we need, saying no can make others become equally productive and focused.

In the following chapter, we will see how interaction among people is essential for the growth of a system, group, or organization.

Core competence

According to Michaelis, inter + action signifies reciprocity between actions, where one influences the other. The adjective effective refers to something concretely manifested through an intended effect. Alternatively, it can describe something adequate, good, or satisfactory. Therefore, we can assert that effective interaction among individuals positively affects how one's actions influence another. What we do affects others, who respond based on their intention.

When I grasped the principle underlying Dr. Goldratt's pillar, people are good; I realized its value in enhancing human potential and fostering constructive relationships, which are essential for the success and evolution of an idea, project, group, family, or institution.

Hence, a need arises to carve out a specific space in the MVS process focused on what I typically refer to as the core competence for achieving common goals: effective interaction.

As we've seen, the belief that people are good fosters understanding, alliances, and buy-in. Especially when executing a plan in communion with people, the quality of our interactions with them will guarantee success in achieving our personal or professional goals.

To successfully achieve a fulfilling life, we must focus on nurturing and developing our interpersonal relationships—how we interact with others. We promote harmony, foster collaboration, and unlock individuals' full potential by strengthening our connections.

However, even considering that 'people are good,' we make mistakes in perceiving the reality around us. We are affected by negative emotions that are in dissonance with the facts. We are tempted to engage in behaviors that damage our relationships and undermine motivation and confidence in our plans.

As Fred Kofman writes in his book Conscious Business, "We tend to see ourselves primarily in the light of our intentions, which are invisible to others, while we see others mainly in the light of their actions which are visible to us." Only the actions are visible, not the intentions, assumptions, or intrinsic needs that drive people to act as they do, including how they express themselves.

We must become aware of the positive impacts our interactions with others can have across various contexts.

Sometimes, we get unproductive and carry out endless discussions with people we care about and know very well, especially when we share a valuable common purpose. Does this sound familiar? What typically happens when we directly blame someone for something? Does it usually lead to acceptance or defense? Depending on the situation, it is normal for responses to become a vicious cycle of defense and attack: I blame you and you, you defend yourself by blaming me, and in defense, I blame you back.

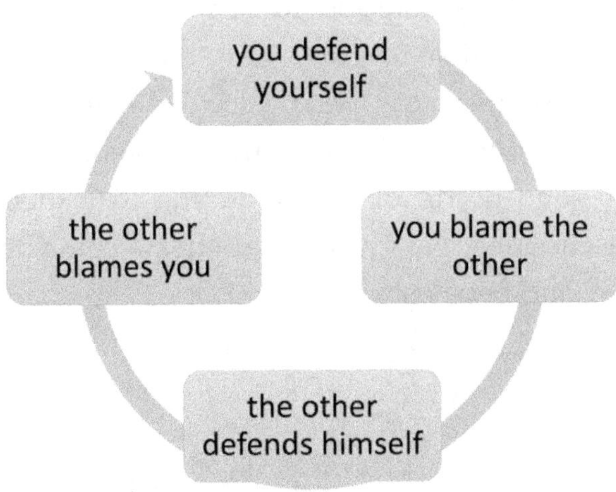

Figure 18 - Vicious Cycle of Defense and Attack

This vicious cycle may occur more softly when people do not exchange defenses and attacks but do not reach a common consensus. One side only tries to defend its point of view, and, in response, the other side continues to defend its own, causing a vicious cycle without the intended result. For instance, people exchange information about themselves without mutual interest. There is no exchange when one is not predisposed to listen to the other actively and vice versa.

When both parties talk over each other, it seems that someone is missing the opportunity to stop and listen. But how is it possible to break this vicious cycle? What communicative skills are missing?

This vicious cycle suggests that no one is trying to understand the other's logic. People do not genuinely listen to each other to grasp how the other feels and thinks. How, then, can persuasion be achieved? How can we convince someone without listening to their thoughts and needs and collaborating with them? We are discussing two cause-and-effect competencies: empathy and persuasion.

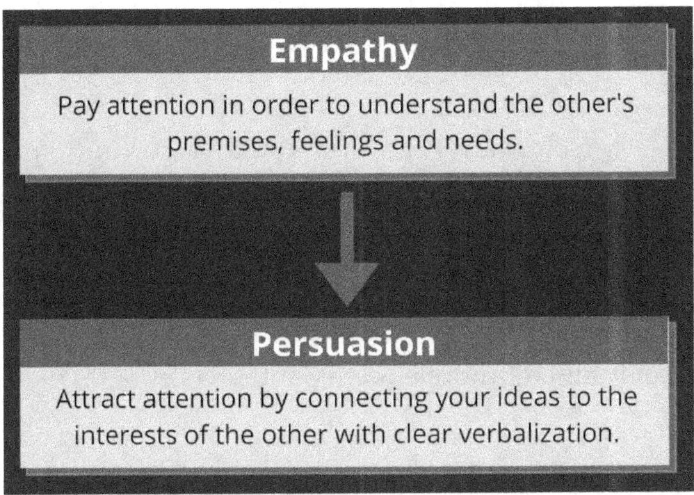

Figure 19 - Effective Interaction

Effective Interaction is composed of two core competencies: empathy and persuasion. I realized that there is a cause-and-effect relationship between these two behavioral competencies. Empathy requires delivering attention, listening, and understanding, while persuasion requires attracting attention, expressing, and convincing.

Inquiring about others' logic is part of practicing empathy. Therefore, it is necessary to listen with full attention and interest firsthand, manifesting understanding and respect for the logic in how the other thinks. Delivering attention attracts the other's attention; it causes alignment instead of resistance. In response, persuasion occurs naturally, as listening first prepares us to connect ideas, shared interests, and needs.

A technical expression common to the field of linguistics is called backchannel. This means responding to what the other says verbally or nonverbally, expressing understanding, interest, and willingness to listen. A simple practice like this can mark the beginning of more effective interaction.

Figure 20 - Effects of Effective Interaction

Empathy and persuasion

Establishing a connection with others is the starting point in practicing persuasion. It's not easy, but it is required if we desire to communicate with people effectively. We practice empathy when we listen to others with the curiosity of someone about to discover something we didn't know. It concerns understanding other premises and perceiving the needs embedded in how others express themselves.

As we pay full attention to others, we receive their attention and respect, which is necessary for developing persuasion.

It's about developing communication skills, even in difficult conversations with opposing opinions. Usually, what happens is an attempt to prove that we are right and the other is wrong, and vice versa. In this way, in addition to wasting a lot of energy and time, we can't solve what we need, damage the relationship, and weaken the common goal.

However, it is possible to succeed by transforming difficult conversations into productive discussions, strengthening bones, and creating opportunities for transformation. When confronted, we cannot control the other, but we can control the process. We need to assume that they are right from their perspective.

Communication becomes difficult if we fail to recognize that the other person is saying something that makes sense to them. We must show that we care about understanding their perspective before trying to defend our ideas. This is no easy task, especially when we are emotionally affected by what we hear. It takes time and practice to become adept at this.

Maintaining clear, positive intentions with the people we interact with daily can be an open-door key.

We can summarize empathy exercise in a few values: respect, understanding, and contribution.

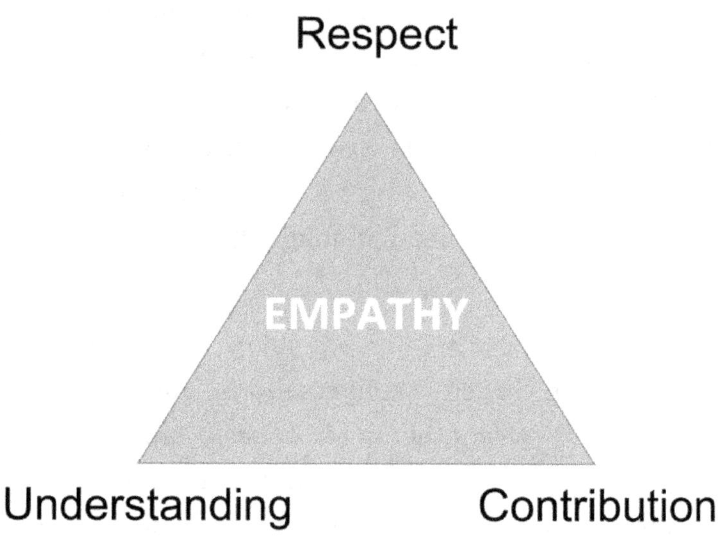

Figure 21 - Values of Empathy

We show respect by recognizing that the other acts based on logic that makes sense to him. We reach an understanding by realizing the other's assumptions and needs that we were unaware of or were not considered. By expressing this understanding, it is possible to generate acceptance and comfort. We can also contribute by asking thoughtful questions, and then the other person reviews premises, validates, or modifies them without feeling judged. It is time to link to what we have to say.

Consequently, persuasion occurs smoothly; we transition from empathy to persuasion subtly and naturally. While engaging in empathetic conversation, we attract attention and align interests, expressing our assumptions and needs to obtain viable win-win solutions without objections.

This process is also valid when considering leadership. Interaction between people is only effective if it yields constructive outcomes.

Every leader who feels responsible for the organization's results fosters effective team interaction, engaging them toward a common purpose. The quality of interactions with teams defines success in making aligned decisions and executing processes that lead to effective results.

Individuals with high growth potential are often dismissed depending on the seriousness of the situation. When the results do not go as planned, there is a tendency to point out blame. We know that blaming exempts us from the responsibility of identifying the hidden causes and finding assertive solutions. Leaders and collaborators who prefer identifying real causes rather than culprits promote professional and business development and growth.

Effective interaction, therefore, impacts the growth of interpersonal relationships. When empathic and persuasive interactions occur in conflicting situations, new ideas arise, building bonds, alignment, learning, and growth.

Sales and new ideas

Selling is not just a salesperson's job. We sell our ideas every time as we interact with others. Therefore, learning to sell should be a compulsory subject in any curriculum.

The empathic approach is to listen first and thus connect our services and products. Therefore, persuasion in the sale occurs naturally, without much effort.

A successful sales approach begins with attentively listening to capture the interests and pain points that align with our service and product solutions. Before asking questions, listening to answers, and detecting needs, trying to persuade with services and products is in vain.

In the book I Hate Selling, Allan Boress indicates that 70% of a sale's success is in listening and asking questions, and 30% is in talking about your product or service. It is necessary to be attentive to the customer, listen to their needs or problems first, understand their reality, and engage in products that serve them.

It is about exercising persuasion through empathy. Interacting with the customer is necessary to generate a reciprocal relationship, sharing values, bonds, and engagement.

Watching Rami Goldratt speak about innovation at the first Goldratt Circle Conference, I heard him talk about innovation and delivering value that impacts our new reality.

We need to adapt to this new reality by listening to and understanding our customers' undesirable effects and providing ideas for disruptive solutions.

Empathy involves accurately reading reality and listening to others to better persuade them about solutions to common problems, whether in the business world or in improving our personal and professional lives.

Effective Interaction is especially relevant when selling new ideas.

What is our expectation of people's reaction when we bring up a great idea that involves them in a shared context? We usually expect the idea to be accepted, and we want to get positive feedback and praise. However, this does not always happen immediately.

We know that every idea, as good as it may seem, if we don't think about negative branches, other people will. And that doesn't necessarily invalidate the idea. As we now know, finding negative branches is an excellent way to refine and improve the idea. However, this premise is not always clear and understood. When someone brings an innovative idea, and someone listens and, when giving feedback, raises something negative, the immediate reaction is to continue defending their idea. At that time, the vicious cycle begins again, where everyone wants to defend their point of view.

Practicing empathy before persuasion helps avoid the unproductive cycle where no one is heard. In this approach, empathy first acknowledges the positive aspects of the idea: it ensures acceptance, shows respect, meets the expectation that a good idea has been generated by someone, and recognizes that intention to resolve or improve a given situation. If we skip the empathy step, the owner of the idea will likely be unable or unprepared to listen to our contributions or objections.

The way we act and react in relationships is logical, based on cause-and-effect logic. Therefore, if we want to attract attention to our objections (persuasion), we must first release attention and explore the other and its positive side (empathy).

Thus, feeling welcomed and valued in their new idea, the person will have much more interest and emotional conditions to pay attention to what we will not call an objection but a contribution. It means preparing the person to understand something that, due to the initial enthusiasm of the idea, they haven't had the chance to understand yet.

On the other hand, when we share new ideas with other people, we must be prepared, and it is natural for someone to realize that something can go wrong. We will benefit greatly if we can do this without taking it personally, reminding people are good. We will have serene reasoning to understand the logic of the objection. Depending on the objection, it could be an opportunity to generate another, better idea.

We constantly try to sell ideas in our family, social, and organizations. Understanding the cause-and-effect relationship that empathy generates on persuasion makes our interactions productive, ensuring harmony and growth in the reality around us.

The layers of resistance to change

It is common to experience resistance to change, even when there is positive evidence and valid needs.

Resistance is common and occurs even when implementing changes will benefit the shared reality of a group or organization.

Assuming that people are good rather than merely stubborn or incompetent, there are substantial reasons why they might resist accepting change. Dr. Goldratt has addressed this issue very accurately, uncovering why people may resist significant change.

He identified six layers that must be overcome step by step.

Even if there is a pot of gold at the end, there is a path to follow to reach it, which may involve adopting a new attitude. It takes us out of our comfort zone or forces us to confront intrinsic fears simply because, deep down, we don't believe that reaching the pot of gold will completely solve the problem or perhaps because we are still unsure about which real problem needs to be solved.

Dr. Eli's six layers of resistance describe a process for overcoming resistance to change, which relies on tools mentioned in the previous chapters, such as the cloud.

1. Agreeing to the problem

When someone is unconvinced about the problem or opportunity, resistance to change can occur. A typical example in one's personal life: I find myself in debt. Will this severely damage my stability in the future? Do I need to change? We resist change when we are not convinced that debt is not a fact of life but a problem that can be avoided. Standards of conduct and other people's values that often seem logical may not be so obvious to you. As Eli Goldratt used to say, "Good sense does not necessarily mean common sense."

2. Agreeing to the direction of the solution

Once everyone agrees on the root cause, which becomes the problem itself, a dilemma usually prevents its solution: get a job with fewer conditions or continue studying for a better opportunity. The cloud tool collaborates to decipher which direction should be followed more clearly.

This example is very simple, but it also adds a lot of value when applied to more complex problems whose dilemma needs to be explained to better convince about the direction of the solution. Agreeing on the direction of the solution is recognizing the logic of the cloud/dilemma and what premise needs to be dropped to evaporate it. Without going through this thinking process, people often try to defend their best interests, which increases resistance to change.

3. Agree that the solution addresses the entire problem

It is necessary to be sure that the defined solution includes all the undesirable effects of the reality to be improved. If we understand the reality well in step one, we will only have to check how the solution will impact those effects for the better.

When you force a solution that leaves out some critical undesirable effect for one of those involved, there is a risk of resistance occurring at a certain point in the implementation. Hence, checking the reality analysis and taking readjustment measures, if necessary, is important to generate a complete solution and ensure everyone entirely agrees with the answer.

4. Yes, but there are negative branches

Everyone agrees, but when implemented, it generates a new undesirable effect. Even in improvement, we must note that other unfavorable effects may arise from change. And an unmissable opportunity arises regarding the solution.

The good news is that anticipating this effect makes it possible to rewire the solution, avoiding even more significant problems than the initial one. For example, the solution worked so well that saving the family from financial debts would involve constant travel, often taking the mother away from her pre-teen children. Therefore, it will be necessary to find solutions that prevent these negative branches, such as accepting the new job and keeping close to the children.

Necessary: When Dr. Eli Goldratt created these layers of resistance, he drew particular attention to these last steps. Many plans fail because they have not considered other effects that can be even more harmful than the problem we are trying to solve. Investing time to generate solutions for the possible negative branches of change must be taken seriously.

From that point, people have already accepted the solution and understood its impact, so they can find contingency measures and protect the execution's success.

5. Yes, but there are obstacles

The brightest solutions may be subject to resistance from someone because obstacles arise to overcome. Such obstacles can be of various natures, such as physical resources, money, environmental, political, human resources, approvals, or behavioral skills.

Time to create measures to avoid or eliminate obstacles without generating other negative effects. Obstacles cannot be omitted; whenever they arise, they must be addressed by sharing them with everyone. There will always be a new action or tactic to overcome them.

When selling an idea or a project, Dr. Eli Goldratt emphasized the importance of having the buyers themselves propose solutions to overcome obstacles. In this stage, it is crucial to recognize that the sale has already been made and allow the buyer to assume the process.

By going too fast to point out solutions, we often miss the chance to involve critical people, trusting their ability to overcome and compromise. This rule applies to the previous item, as well, when we give space for those who are being persuaded to work out ways to reverse possible negative branches. Therefore, we will ensure people buy into the idea when we offer people opportunities to generate solutions rather than always imposing the answers.

6. Non-verbalized fears

Another factor that may be the reason for resistance to change is fears or deep paradigms, which are not apparent in principle, that make the person change his mind at the last minute, even after all preparation and even after having a safe plan to face the change.

Dr. Eli Goldratt used to quote the paratrooper analogy. Even after hours of theoretical and practical preparation, a lot of waiting, and the certainty of realizing his dream at the right time, a resistance coming from his intuition, which does not usually ask for permission, makes him stop his hands on the plane door in movement, rather than using the door as outward thrust support. When it comes to the first jump, it usually takes a "little help" from the instructor, who suddenly pushes him out and lets the skydiver discover the safety he needs in the act.

This tactic can be used in other situations when someone encourages you or reminds you of the deal, the benefits of change, or new achievements. But it is also possible to discover what dilemma prevents you from realizing your dream of changing.

Often, it is a simple paradigm that needs to be broken. I will cite a practical example of a healthcare professional client who was about to launch her own business and needed to break the paradigm of getting referrals from clients. She had to ask for a favor, calling her contacts.

When she realized that her physiotherapy work would solve a significant limitation of her contacts, the professional exchanged thoughts and feelings within herself: "I will not be asking for a favor. On the contrary, I will offer help and support to the patients of my contacts."

Resistance to change is not necessarily bad. It is very effective in persuading ideas that involve groups of people in search of improvement in a situation that affects them, whether of a family, institutional or organizational nature. It could be the opportunity to refine the solution and an excellent interpersonal alignment tool.

Whatever the purpose, overcoming the layers of resistance reinforces the practice of effective interaction between people, strengthening bonds, building alliances, and fostering collaboration. The art of convincing shifts to the ability to listen and generate responses that facilitate the implementation of a change and ensure successful completion.

CHAPTER VIII – CONTINUOUS IMPROVEMENT

Stamina and course corrections

Each week, review your accomplishments and move forward with focus! Ask for feedback mid-implementation if needed. But don't give up on the first obstacle because it will happen. Believe in your ability to overcome and always find win-win solutions.

Feedback provides an opportunity to assess what is working well and what is not. What should be changed if mistakes occur, and what should be added to or eliminated from the plan as we move forward? Therefore, the roadmap is dynamic. You must review it with the real intention of protecting the flow toward your purpose.

Stamina: Athletes develop resistance to maintain themselves in a situation of great effort for a long time, as they desire to achieve their most important purpose in a competition. When a climber's dream is to reach the top of Everest, this condition governs the entire process of developing stamina to make their dream come true. This capacity for resistance is called stamina. Stamina can be physical or emotional; I believe the two influence each other.

Emotional stimulation, such as the feeling of realizing a dream, the self-confidence in achieving it, or when someone manifests trust in their employees, can trigger the release of neurotransmitters that positively impact performance.

Therefore, stamina becomes an indicator that keeps us moving toward our purpose in life's trials. This ability to stay on course in our dreams, nurtured by a meaningful goal, keeps us from giving up.

If you hesitate to move on by chance, it's time to remember your reasons and the decision to persist. You must review your feelings and understand the cause of your resistance. Sharing with the right people will also help you get back on course. Therefore, you must align the plan with everyone involved, seeking collaboration and commitment when the plan depends on others to succeed. Aligning means checking understanding and making small changes to adapt to others when necessary.

Here is the true meaning of a full life - one where we will always see opportunities for improvement and have certainty in our ability to reach them. We feel like we're always moving forward, living in continuous growth. This prevents setbacks and keeps us prepared for possible adversities along the way.

Stabilization or stagnation?

Some people confuse stagnation with stability.

Once we stop thinking about new challenges for growth and advancement, whether, in the personal area or our projects, there is an excellent risk of stagnation because after reaching the level of satisfaction we aim for, it is time to enjoy the new reality only. After all, we fought so hard to get where we are. The problem is that stagnation, stopping thinking about the facts, inhibits the view of growth and can lead to setbacks.

Reality changes. Nothing is static. Circumstances change, the market reacts, science advances, the economy changes, people mature, our children grow up, and history surprises us with different reactions. These dynamics move our imagination, dreams, and awareness of life.

I believe that, even without intention, human beings are constantly transforming themselves as they need to adapt.

It reinforces the importance of remaining aware of what matters to us, such as values and our personal influence and contribution - our personal purpose. With that North Star, we will not be so vulnerable to destabilizing circumstances.

When we are not fully aware of ourselves and our reality, we often get carried away by reactions, habits, and values that do not serve us and do not generate good results.

We need to be increasingly aware of our growth potential. In this way, we will undoubtedly be protagonists of a constantly flourishing life in which we make an impact.

Our behavioral competencies and skills improve as we live if we are personally attentive. We are gaining experience and learning from it. It defines our maturity. Therefore, it is natural that our potential for advancement and achievement also increases. What would be the limit of that capacity? How can we set a limit, or why set a limit? What are we protecting ourselves from if we have a clear purpose and values that guide us?

Intentional humility of growth

Never say I already know.

It is the fourth pillar of the TOC mindset.

Assuming we don't always know everything about the best solution to situations increases our willingness and openness to check our assumptions and reality. Thus, the chances of discovering better solutions also increase significantly.

As we gain experience, we acquire self-sufficiency from all the learning. However, the reality is constantly changing. We risk stopping to check reality and challenge the assumptions arising from previous experiences, which still guide our current actions and decision-making.

For this reason, the key is knowing how to challenge – the basic principle of learning how to think clearly. When challenging the premises that support a decision or situation, we find disruptive solutions that allow growth.

Scientists are naturally in the habit of thinking in this humble state of always looking to know more, not assuming they already know everything. They assume doubts and failures with the certainty that they have mastered a path, a method to unveil what has not yet been seen.

Hope is always willing to discover a new possibility.

For improvement and growth, not even the sky is the limit.

Any system can be substantially improved, however suitable because it won't stay that way forever.

Like everything in life, nothing happens if we don't take the first step. Improvement is often intuitive. People are usually looking to improve something, from their health, energy, quality of life, business, financial planning, and relationships.

Continuously and systemically examining our context and understanding the cause-and-effect relationships among its elements give us clarity on the next root cause to address, recognizing that it may change over time.

Once we see the desirable effects of a change, it's time to identify the next point of improvement and continue this process throughout our lives. Herein lies a life of continuous growth.

There is a simple way to practice this ongoing improvement process with awareness, validating, and refining your intuition and emotion, which indicate signs of a truth that cannot be neglected or postponed.

A-The practice is to create a space and a time periodically. It could be a special day, a weekend, in a calm and fancy place, in nature, or in the comfort of your home. It can be twice a year, four times a year, or every two months.

B-Invite those you are involved with and possibly have common goals, primarily spouses, relatives, and children. The exercise can be done individually, but I assure you that team sharing adds joy and enriches the commitment and support. You may invite your business partners or colleagues if the relationship is very close and trusting.

C- Review the results obtained around the implemented plans so far. Recognize what worked, what was accomplished, and how it impacted other areas of life: family, emotional, financial, leisure, health, or others.

D- List what makes you grateful. It includes facts, achievements, and people who participated in your story.

E- Decide if there are people to send a message of thanks, which is very important. Maybe it's an opportunity to validate other important people and invite them closer.

F- After having a broad vision of significant improvement, you will see your reality differently. Other effects may have arisen along the way. It is time to define again what your next improvement challenge is and predict how the result of this change will impact your purpose and reality.

What if the results work out better than expected? What other effects can be predicted?

Once you improve your reality, don't allow inertia to stop you.

Review your purpose. Find out the next opportunity to grow. Now you know the process!

Mindset summary

To live fully is to live with meaning and purpose, a state that brings us the long-awaited happiness we seek.

- Reality is simple in the way it works.

- Any situation, however good it may be, can be significantly improved; not even the sky is the limit.

- If there is no harmony, it means that something should be changed.

- Everyone can live a Full Life.

What do these principles lead us to think?

What experiences come to mind?

What are we passionate about?

What do we want to change in the world?

Whatever the complexity of the situation, institution, community, or company in which we operate, if we apply these principles above and try to respond to them, it is quite possible that innovative goals will surface.

Identifying ambitious goals is also a way of bringing meaning to life. It doesn't matter whether they are on the verge of solving a massive problem involving the planet or simply a personal challenge. What matters is that they ignite passion in your heart.

We all have the potential to live a full life. Living a full life involves exploring our potential. It enhances our values, desires, ambitions, and purposes for the greater good, transcending what we see around us.

Every person who dedicates themselves to living a full life, directly and indirectly, impacts thousands of people.

I believe everyone who dedicates themselves to personal growth also contributes to others creating a better world.

CHAPTER IX – HOW I USE MVS IN COACHING PROCESSES

The differential that TOC adds to coaching

Coaching is traditionally defined as a form of development in which a trained professional or coach, supports a client, the coachee, in achieving a specific personal or professional goal by providing training and guidance.

"If I have seen further, it is by standing upon the shoulders of giants." (Isaac Newton, 1675)

The expression "upon the shoulders of giants" was sometimes used by Dr. Goldratt, urging the world to think scientifically and extending the applications of the Theory of Constraints to other areas where it could contribute.

After experiencing my own transformation via TOC, I knew how what I learned could contribute to coaching and how I could help others significantly improve their lives and find their purpose.

Next, I will resume the most significant contributions of Theory of Constraints (TOC) applied to the coaching process.

The clarity in what to change

Over nearly a decade in the profession, I have had the opportunity to work alongside professionals, executives, and entrepreneurs who were striving to improve. Helping them clearly see their reality and precisely understand - what to change - is the key differentiator of the coaching process, which is supported by the Theory of Constraints.

In the traditional coaching process, usually, the client must decide what they believe needs to be improved the most, as several competencies emerge as opportunities after analysis conducted by the coach. And this agrees with the logic that we are naturally capable but often suffer the influence of our predisposition to change something. Therefore, after a few sessions, it is customary to realize that what you decide to develop is not precisely what will make a difference. What happens is that perhaps the first choice was not so well founded. TOC's thinking process makes it possible within a scientific approach to analyze facts from the perspective of cause-and-effect logic, considering thoughts, emotions, and behaviors.

Definition of focus

A paradigm to be broken is the belief that improving everything that can be improved signifies high performance. Trying to improve everything at once can expend much effort for minimal results due to a dispersion of focus.

TOC offers a distinctive approach. Once the priority is defined, it focuses on the specific area that impacts the overall objective, specifically targeting the constraint that hinders overall performance. Focus means subordinating every decision to this primary concern, which also involves deciding what not to do.

After achieving the desired results, it is time to expand the goal and progress to the next significant leap.

Conflict solution

Another aspect TOC brings to coaching is addressing dilemmas and conflicts as an intelligence skill in relationships. Instead of merely managing dilemmas, TOC aims to eliminate them whenever they impair the performance of reality.

As we have seen previously, systemic dilemmas or interpersonal conflicts must be accurately addressed, as they present opportunities for improvement by figuring out solutions that eliminate them. Conflicts must be eliminated, not managed, whenever there is a common goal. An effective tool for this purpose is the cloud technique.

This disruptive tool fosters emotional intelligence when dealing with interpersonal conflicts. The cloud technique prevents us from judging while promoting empathy. Rather than judging, it provides solutions that allow both sides to win.

Based on transparency, collaboration is possible in a way that helps people recognize incorrect assumptions and change attitudes or actions that conflict with others. It is not possible to change people, but it is possible to enhance their thinking and improve their perceptions of themselves, others, and reality.

Mindset acquisition

Another contribution that TOC brings to coaching processes is acquiring a mindset during the process that does not end with reaching the current goal. The process via TOC is supported by a clear and defined mindset that provides a lifetime of development. The 4 Pillars described in Chapter II start managing the flow on a daily basis. It significantly improves the decision-making, relationships, communication skills, and ability to generate win-win solutions, among other competencies that will be presented further. Once an individual learns throughout the process, this new mindset is incorporated for a lifetime benefit.

An example with comparative methods

To better understand the TOC differential, I present the same example of a real case conducted in a traditional coaching session and then in the TOC version.

The context: the client was a partner of an IT company and was uncomfortable with his day-to-day situation in the company. They performed the service directly at the customers' companies and had a team of four technicians.

The traditional coaching session would trigger a dialogue like the one below in the initial ongoing phase:

-Coach: What bothers you right now?

-Coachee: I'm worried about our performance because, among many assignments, my partner and I have a severe problem managing the schedule.

-Coach: And if you managed the schedule correctly, what would that bring you?

-Coachee: It would bring more clarity, and we wouldn't get in the way of serving customers more quickly. At the same time, we would be more available to solve the complications that threaten the quality of delivery.

-Coach: I see this is very important for the company and the results you want.

-Coachee: Certainly.

(At this point, after better describing the company's day-to-day, some competencies needing improvement would emerge).

-Coach: To achieve what you need, what do we have an opportunity to develop here? Which of these skills that emerged do you think you need to build more?

-Coachee: Productivity. To be more productive.

-Coach: Right. What are the universal characteristics of someone productive?

From that moment, the Coach would lead the development of the behavioral competence that the client suggested. And yes, maybe I could organize the schedule more productively.

Now, I describe how the process was conducted via TOC. Note: The dialogs in this method are summarized.

-Coach: What bothers you right now?

-Coachee: I'm worried about our performance because, among many assignments, my partner and I have a serious problem managing the schedule.

- Coach: Yes. And what changes if you get it?

-Coachee: It would bring more clarity, and we wouldn't get in the way of serving customers more quickly. At the same time, we would be more available to solve the complications that threaten the quality of delivery.

- Coach: Yes. I can see that you are concerned with aligning the company's operations with service and, at the same time, obtaining more quality in delivering the service, right?

- Coachee: Perfect.

Coach: By validating whether it is a matter of agenda, we can get a complete view of reality.

- Coachee: How so?

- Coach: You can raise all the undesirable effects that have been occurring in the company and understand the root cause. It could check the processes, the roles of the partners and profiles, the team, and the company results as a result of these factors. What do you think?

- Coachee: It would be very interesting. Maybe the cause of the problem is something else.

- Coach: Exactly. You need to understand what needs to change first to improve reality systemically.

- Coachee: Yes, I want to do that.

Next, the client raised the undesirable effects that bothered him:

1- The operational processes are not clear.

2- The members' day-to-day roles are not clearly defined.

3- We don't have time to develop new potential customers.

4- The team gives us problems when the situation has already become severe.

5- We are overloaded with customer complications.

6- We were unable to manage the schedule.

7- The closing of new contracts stopped.

8- Billing is at risk.

The client verbalized the undesirable effects after understanding the dynamics from the perspective of the logic applied through tools. Then, he put it in the order above, understanding the cause-and-effect relationship.

By applying the cause-and-effect principle, reality emerged without the slightest intention of pointing out solutions, and the customer could see the entire system had compromised performance.

Just as a doctor diagnoses to identify the root cause to focus on treatment, a coach probes the client's real symptoms and uses scientific methods to ask questions the client might not consider. This approach helps the client broaden his vision and clarify what to change first.

Just organizing the agenda to optimize time would not solve the client's primary goal of improving their performance in the company. The most significant performance risk was in the company's commercial area, which needed immediate attention then.

The client decided it was urgent to focus on enhancing the relationship with its commercial executive and improving sales skills. Roles, human resources, processes, and finally, the priority-based agenda for everyone were all improvement decisions subordinate to the ultimate goal: closing new contracts.

In addition to more organization and discipline on the agenda, a new focus element has emerged, the essential element for accelerating results and productivity. As a result, the development focus was directed toward achieving better results in sales, and the coaching process continued to awaken best practices and skills based on successful experiences that have already occurred. They added this learning to the best sales techniques on the market and adapted to the reality they knew and mastered so well – the market and the IT service.

The coaching process tripled the company's revenue, avenging four prospects in the drawer. This focus organized the company as a whole, clarifying which activities to prioritize and which to discontinue to pursue their unified purpose.

From then on, the organization of the agenda became manageable. It resulted from the priorities aligned between the partners and was no longer the result of individual competence. After that, the client developed other competencies but focused on the real problem that had to be solved to bring about significant results: communicating with the team, effectively delegating, and selling.

The principle of cause and effect goes beyond making the right decisions for change and helps to understand the dilemmas and conflicts that arise along the way and that prevent or hinder the plan's success.

With the follow-up and quick feedback loop, coaching via the TOC process significantly collaborates to resolve these dilemmas and conflicts, often of a personal or technical nature.

Behavioral skills and the four pillars

Whether in the business or personal development, necessary skills guarantee efficiency in execution. It is during execution that we experience behavioral competencies that facilitate the achievement of results and daily journeys.

These competencies below are addressed once individuals learn and start applying the four pillars that sustain the mindset of TOC through the processes of coaching.

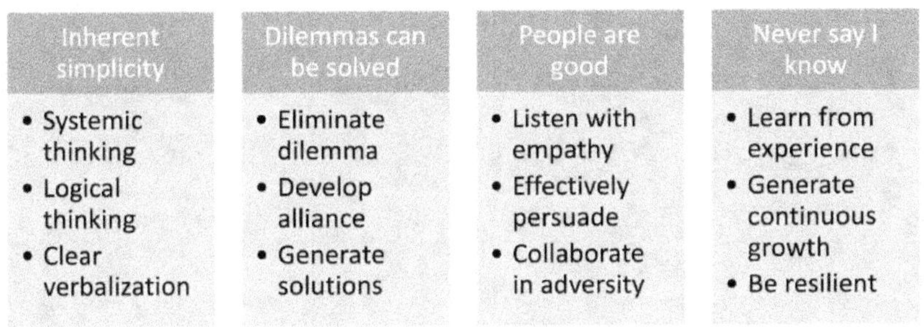

Figure 22 - Competencies

These competencies assure success and enhance personal relationships. Additionally, this development process fosters renewal thinking.

In coaching processes, the role of a coach is to rationalize questions systematically through a structured methodology. This enables the clients to decipher reality and gain the clarity needed to discover and implement their own solutions. The TOC mindset, tools, and fundamentals comprise a robust methodology that really impacts coaching precisely by delivering long-term improvement.

CHAPTER X: CASES IN DIFFERENT CIRCUMSTANCES

A driver who changed his life – reading the book

My husband, Aureo Villagra, was on a business trip for his company when he took an Uber and struck up a casual conversation with the driver. The driver shared the challenges he was facing, and he was confused about his plans for the future. At the end of the ride, Aureo asked if the young man enjoyed reading and if he would accept the first edition of this book as a gift, suggesting it could help. The driver took the offer and later received the book at the specified address.

After several months without contact and having nearly forgotten the episode, Aureo received the following message on his Instagram:

"Just dropping by to say thanks. Last year, we were on an Uber ride, and you gave me the book 'Think Clearly, Act with Focus'. It was precious for the phase of life I was going through. I had so many things to address at once, and I was overwhelmed with work as I juggled Uber and managing my store. My family was in disarray, facing financial troubles, and no matter how hard I tried, I didn't see any results.The first time I read the book, I couldn't quite grasp how to pinpoint the root cause of all my troubles. I always thought my situation was too complicated, so it was impossible to have such a straightforward solution. However, upon reading it a second time, I could comprehend and began to analyze my own life. I realized I was directing my efforts in the wrong areas. Now, I no longer drive for Uber. My wife and I work together in the store, and my marriage is better than ever, especially since she helps me manage. This circumstance gives me time to focus on my studies. I've set up a makeshift office within my store where I oversee and act as a traffic manager for local businesses. For now, I'm working on launching my own product in the coming months."

This story was enriching. One of my goals with this book is to allow individuals unfamiliar with coaching techniques or TOC to gain insights that help them lead more meaningful lives.

A big company in Brazil – using it in a leadership alignment project

The founding partner and CEO of a big company in Brazil had been introduced to TOC. Still, they had never implemented it in his firm because they prioritized partnership matters with international investors, which consumed his managerial attention.

He read the book over a weekend and gave a striking testimony, stating it ranked among the best books he had ever read.

He realized it was time to implement TOC in the company. Still, he chose the approach based on the MVS: first, his directors would undergo the process, and upon seeing results in their reality, they would be more inclined to apply TOC throughout the company.

He then decided to hire coaching services with the MVS method for the entire leadership team, including himself, initially on an individual basis. A kick-off meeting in the form of a workshop was held with the CEO and the seven directors of the main departments to align everyone with the project's objectives and introduce the methodology.

Next, I began implementing Phase I of the MVS - Think Clearly: Full Consciousness, Inherent Simplicity, and Solution Direction. After about two months, individual feedback meetings were scheduled between each of the Directors and the CEO, with my oversight, to discuss any insights they felt relevant about what the MVS process brought to their personal side and how that could align with the company's objectives and values.

However, they most spontaneously shared the plans developed during the individual processes. They mentioned what it brought to their personal lives, especially in redefining their personal purpose, how it connected to their professional side, and how it was compatible with the company's values and goals. The day was concluded with a two-hour workshop in which the CEO validated the company's strategic plan to all involved leaders and departments. Furthermore, all participants could acknowledge each other and understand each other's potential and needs. They then identified ways to collaborate between their areas of expertise towards a common and clear objective, even though there was competition for the CEO's succession in some cases.

Cancer surgery – using it as a TOC expert

While this book was in its final stage for the first edition, Aureo discovered during a routine checkup that he had esophageal cancer stemming from a hiatal hernia that was harming the esophagus with gastric acid. It was tiny as it was in the early stages but, at the same time, very aggressive; it could be fatal shortly after growing further.

Therefore, the appropriate treatment was surgery to remove the esophagus and part of the stomach. There were three possible scenarios: dying during the surgery, surviving but then needing an aggressive chemotherapy and radiotherapy treatment if metastasis had already occurred, or being fully cured.

After our initial shock, he decided it was time to make the best possible decisions using the TOC Thinking Processes. He was also already familiar with this book's insights. He used these insights to prepare a Strategy and Tactic Tree (S&T) for what he termed a 'life leverage point', given that so much could change. The S&T is the same tool he uses to manage projects with his consulting clients.

In this way, he organized his thoughts and plans on preparing for surgery, returning to everyday life, and undergoing a genuine learning process in each scenario. If he didn't make it, at least there would be lessons for the family.

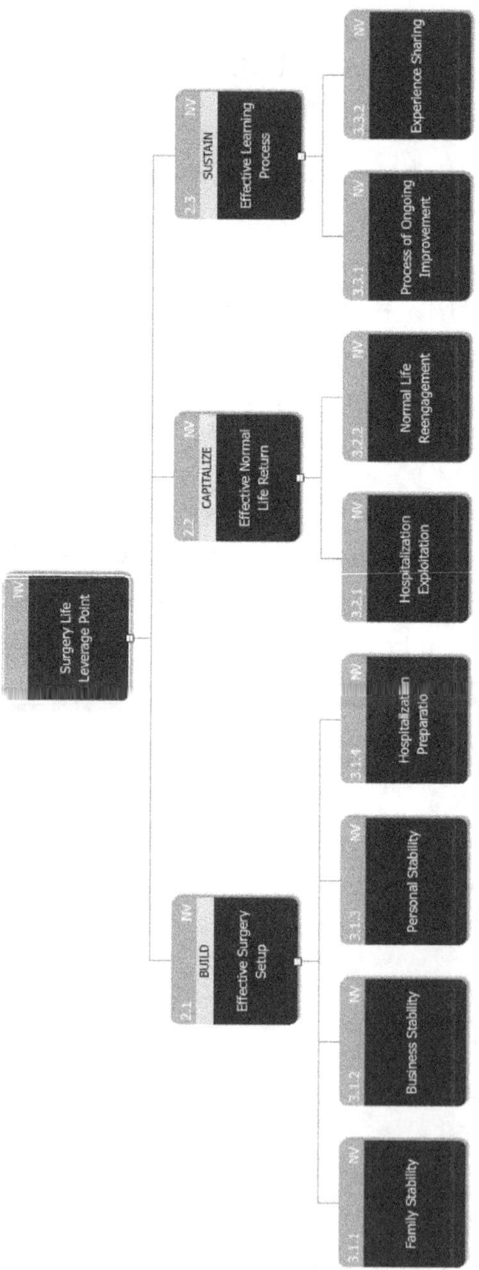

Figure 23 – Cancer S&T

The plan included preparing his family, the company where he is the CEO of one of the operations, and himself to handle all possible scenarios.

The surgery was a success. My husband didn't need any additional treatment, and due to the stomach reduction that occurred, he lost over 45 pounds and is now much healthier than before.

As anticipated in the final part of his S&T, we periodically apply the learning process we established as a couple. We even conducted a Proof of Concept at a philanthropic institution that houses cancer patients undergoing lengthy treatments at one of the largest cancer hospitals in Latin America.

The patients' financial and logistical aspects were sorted. However, the psychological aspect of those who sometimes needed to spend over a year away from home, away from their jobs, and family still needed to be addressed. The idea was to use the patients' available time and guide them through the process, helping them draft their goals for returning to everyday life after treatment. Spreading hope is a noble mission in moments of adversity, and this TOC volunteer application is an idea we plan to explore further.

Today, Aureo shares his story in conferences and in his daily life to inspire others to see the Thinking Processes of TOC as something that can genuinely change lives.

What do these cases have in common?

1- People involved assumed responsibility for their lives (not victims).
2- They did not stay alone and went in search of help.
3- They accepted help and support.
4- They believed in the process.
5- They followed the implementation of their decisions and plans.
6- They achieved success and kept learning with experience.

Conclusion quote:

"I smile and start to count on my fingers. One, people are good. Two, every conflict can be removed. Three, every situation, no matter how complex it initially looks, it is exceedingly simple. Four, every situation can be substantially improved; even the sky is not the limit. Five, every person can reach a full life. Six, there is always a win-win solution. Shall I continue to count?"

Dr. Eli Goldratt – The Choice

CHAPTER XI – NEUROSCIENCE

My deep-rooted passion for personal growth has ignited my curiosity about its potential implications for exploring the TOC approach to improving the brain's capabilities.

I continued my studies by attending an MIT Neuroscience for Business program in 2024. Reading the book of the neuroscientist responsible for developing the program, I dropped in these words right on the first page:

"Neuroscientist Dr. Tara Swart is convinced that we all have the power to lead the lives we want. That's because the things we most wish for - health, happiness, wealth, love - are not governed by mysterious forces, but by our ability to think, feel, and act; in other words, by our brains." (Tara Swart, The Source)

By extending the above thinking, TOC teaches that the things we wish for in life are governed by a few causes since all the elements that compose our lives are interconnected in a cause-and-effect logic, which is mostly our ability to think clearly, feel, and act accordingly.

This chapter will share some important neuroscience fundamentals regarding mastering our brain efficiency to achieve our desired lives. I humbly express my happiness in concluding how the MVSystem can contribute and adapt to neuroscience applications.

Stage 1- Full Consciousness

Recognizing the life story and be grateful

In the "Full Consciousness" first stage of the MVS method, recognizing our life stories and practicing gratitude are emphasized as fundamental tools for self-knowledge and building self-confidence. These exercises promote emotional well-being and have solid foundations in neuroscience, showing how they can positively influence brain function.

Recognizing and reflecting on our life stories helps us better understand our experiences, decisions, and personal characteristics. This process of self-reflection is directly linked to brain functions in areas responsible for memory and emotional processing, such as the hippocampus and amygdala.

Self-reflection and personal narrative activate the medial prefrontal cortex, which processes self-related information. Studies show that reflecting on personal experiences can strengthen autobiographical memory and improve self-understanding, essential for developing self-knowledge.

Moreover, the practice of gratitude has been extensively studied in neuroscience and is proven to offer emotional and cognitive benefits. Feeling and expressing gratitude can activate brain circuits associated with pleasure and reward and promote the release of neurotransmitters such as dopamine and serotonin, which are linked to well-being.

Gratitude activates the brain's reward system, which is crucial for the sensation of pleasure. Research indicates that regular gratitude practices can increase neural activity in brain areas responsible for motivation and action, improving mood and overall life satisfaction.

Engaging in regular gratitude practices and recognition of life achievements can influence neuroplasticity, the brain's ability to form new neural connections and reorganize itself throughout life. When you consciously reflect on your experiences, especially challenging ones, and find aspects to be grateful for, your brain strengthens the neural pathways that foster resilience, positivity, and self-confidence, especially when recognizing your abilities to overcome problems.

Therefore, promoting self-knowledge and the appreciation of achievements can activate brain circuits that enhance emotional states.

Have a purpose

Determining a purpose involves aligning our deepest, most meaningful intentions with the lives we desire; it is about finding pathways to make our dreams a reality. In other words, living a purpose-oriented life awakens our motivation and fosters a more positive mindset.

"By consciously bringing our desires, hopes, and dreams to the forefront of our mind, our brain will be able to home more effectively on opportunities that will lead to the outcomes we want. (Tara Swart – The Source)

Thinking and interacting with people and situations have significant neurochemical effects on the brain and body. Individuals who are unaware of their purposes and potential tend to be more vulnerable to adversities and negative events. Lacking awareness of what drives them daily, they are more susceptible to negative thoughts, which trigger stress responses by increasing cortisol and adrenaline in the blood, ultimately impacting their immunity.

It is noteworthy that athletes, competitors, volunteers, leaders, and employees driven by meaningful purposes nurture more positive goals and are more motivated to overcome challenges.

Moreover, neuroscientists affirm that our brains experience a neurochemical effect when we are purpose-driven and live in environments where trust is prevalent, largely due to the production of oxytocin, most known as the 'bonding hormone'.

Stage 2- Inherent Simplicity

Inherent Simplicity, one of the pillars of the Theory of Constraints (TOC), teaches us that a system's operation is fundamentally simple despite its apparent complexity. This concept is crucial for understanding how the human brain can operate more efficiently, especially when associated with the Current Reality Tree (CRT) tool.

Neuroscience reveals that the brain constantly seeks patterns and simplicity to conserve energy and increase efficiency. This principle aligns with the Inherent Simplicity stage, which proposes that focusing on a specific root cause can resolve multiple undesirable effects, avoiding the dispersion of efforts on superficial and isolated solutions.

This approach reflects how our brain functions most efficiently. By reducing cognitive overload and focusing on simple, strategic solutions, we can free up mental resources for more creative and innovative tasks. The Current Reality Tree (CRT) facilitates simplifying complexity and directing attention to what truly matters, enabling our brain to work more focused and productively, promoting mental clarity and better decision-making.

The concept of focus is paramount in optimizing brain efficiency, significantly impacting emotional stress and anxiety. Neuroscientific research underscores that maintaining focus can streamline cognitive processes, enhancing overall brain performance.

From a neuroscience standpoint, focus helps the brain allocate resources more effectively. The prefrontal cortex, responsible for executive functions such as decision-making, attention, and problem-solving, plays a critical role in maintaining focus. When we concentrate on a specific task, the brain reduces the noise from irrelevant stimuli, enabling more efficient processing and improved performance.

Focusing on a defined goal can mitigate emotional stress and anxiety. When the brain is overloaded with multiple stimuli or tasks, it can lead to cognitive fatigue and increased stress levels. We can reduce this overload by narrowing our focus and promoting a sense of control and calmness.

Focus is not only about immediate cognitive efficiency but also plays a crucial role in long-term brain health and adaptability, known as neuroplasticity. This process is vital for learning, memory, and recovery from brain injuries.

This alignment shows that focusing on what truly matters can improve mental clarity, emotional stability, and overall cognitive function, ultimately contributing to a more meaningful and fulfilling life.

Stage 3- Direction of the Solution

Every dilemma can be eliminated. This principle underscores that challenging and changing one's assumptions can open new avenues for thinking and problem-solving, thereby facilitating the restoration of harmony.

The 'evaporating the cloud' thinking process fosters cognitive flexibility, developing the mental ability to toggle between different concepts and perspectives simultaneously. This approach is instrumental in awakening creative thinking when assessing both sides of the dilemma and crafting innovative solutions. Therefore, this approach bridges logical thinking to creative thinking.

"Creativity is the ability to shape your brain by what you expose it to, see patterns where they are not obvious, and join the dots in a novel way, designing your future and taking action to make it happen." (Swart, 2019)

The Theory of Constraints also regards intuition as an important aspect of analyzing situations, forming assumptions, and applying logic to them.

Dr. Tara Swart emphasizes the importance of utilizing diverse thinking in our organization, exploring different brain areas, such as logical thinking, mastering emotions, developing intuition, and creative thinking.

Regarding mastering emotions, resolving important dilemmas or conflicts enhances the ability to manage negative thoughts and feelings. It improves our emotional state by preventing the accumulation of unexpressed negative feelings that often occur when we live with unresolved dilemmas daily, merely managing instead of solving them. I am confident that this can alleviate stress, regulating cortisol levels that impact cognitive functions such as memory and attention.

Attention plays a crucial role in productivity while following sustainable solutions. It helps us clarify our thoughts, decisions, and actions.

In summary, this thinking process offers a structured approach to clear thinking that aligns with neuroscience insights about how brain functionality and optimization impact the brain-body connection.

The Future Reality Tree

The science of visualization involves providing tools that facilitate the brain's ability to pre-experience the future, even promoting physical sensations. This becomes a powerful method for activating pathways in our brains. Dr. Tara Swart suggests building an 'action board' with pictures representing what we have defined to achieve in the future.

When we design our Future Reality Tree (FRT), we effectively create a pre-visualization diagram of an ideal future. This diagram clearly identifies the focus aspect—the root cause at the bottom—that will make it happen.

"Another advantage of visualizing the future outcomes you want is that this can raise any potential barriers or obstacles to your success from non-conscious to conscious in your brain. Once you know what these might be, you can preempt or even overturn them if they happen in real life." (Swart– MIT program – Neuroscience for Business, 2024)

Similarly, the Future Reality Tree (FRT) tool also involves identifying potential obstacles that could prevent us from succeeding and transforming them into intermediate actions to overcome them. The FRT enables us - and our brains - to become aware of these barriers and anticipate solutions.

Stage 4 - Focused Execution

Dr. Daniel Levitin is one of the foremost scientists who emphasizes managing and reducing distractions to maintain cognitive efficiency and well-being. Levitin stresses the importance of an organized physical and digital environment. Clutter can be a significant distraction that consumes our attentional resources, so maintaining a tidy, organized workspace can help minimize cognitive load.

He suggests controlling when and how you access information. For example, checking emails and social media at designated times rather than constantly throughout the day can help reduce interruptions and maintain focus.

Prioritizing tasks based on importance and urgency can help manage attention more effectively. Levitin recommends using tools like to-do lists and calendars not just for appointments but to block out time for uninterrupted work on priority projects.

Technology should enhance productivity, not detract from it. Levitin advises setting up appropriate filters and notifications and using apps that help maintain focus and organize tasks.

Avoid Multitasking

Dr. Daniel Levitin discusses the drawbacks of multitasking and its impact on the brain. While multitasking might create the illusion of productivity, Levitin emphasizes that it often diminishes output. His research indicates that multitasking can disrupt the formation of memories. Focused, undivided attention is essential for transferring information from short-term to long-term memory. Multitasking hinders this process, leading to more superficial learning and poorer recall. Additionally, multitasking can elevate stress hormones such as cortisol and adrenaline, overstimulating the brain and leading to disorganized thinking. Levitin argues that this increased stress response not only affects mental health but also impairs the brain's ability to perform tasks effectively.

Define Habits

From a physiological standpoint, taking care of the brain requires adopting some key habits, according to neuroscience. These practices are essential if we aim to optimize brain efficiency and improve our performance and outcomes, as follows:

1.   Resting: numerous studies indicate good sleep positively impacts cognition and memory. During sleep, the glymphatic system – which involves glial cells

in the brain - requires 7-8 hours to flux out toxins that accumulate during the day from various sources, such as processed food, stress, and alcohol. These toxins are responsible for causing degenerative brain diseases. (Tara Swart – The Source)

2.	Fueling: Our brain makes up only 2 percent of our body weight, yet it consumes 25-30 percent of the nutrients we ingest, and it cannot store fuel for later use. Hunger significantly impacts decision-making. A healthy and balanced diet rich in protein, whole grains (amino acids), and 'good fats' is recommended to protect the brain's health. (Tara Swart - The Source)

3.	Hydrating: The brain is approximately 78 percent water. A 1-3 percent decrease in hydration levels can negatively impact our focus, attention, and memory. (Tara Swart - The Source)

4.	Oxygenating: Regular exercise has many benefits for the brain. We breathe more deeply, which oxygenates cells throughout our body. It improves neuroplasticity and supports learning and memory functions. Aerobic exercise has various mental benefits, such as reducing stress and anxiety and increasing confidence. On a neurochemical level, aerobic exercise reduces the release of stress hormones cortisol and adrenalin and stimulates the production of endorphins, which are chemicals responsible for relieving stress and pain. (Tara Swart -The Source)

Understanding how stress and anxiety can interfere with our thinking processes is crucial in improving decision-making and enhancing the quality of our relationships – two key factors for successful plan execution.

Stage 5 - Effective Interaction

Chapter VII explores how empathy involves both emotional and logical elements, understanding and respecting others' thoughts and feelings from their perspective. This process helps individuals connect more deeply with others, facilitating more effective communication and conflict resolution.

This principle is effectively demonstrated when the cloud technique is applied to resolve conflicts between two parts: one side listens to and understands the thoughts (assumptions) behind the needs and actions of the other part, and vice versa. This mutual understanding leads to win-win solutions and fosters deeper alignment between individuals.

Effective interaction suggests genuine listening is essential for persuading and establishing a successful connection with individuals, especially when facing controversial scenarios.

The third pillar of the Theory of Constraints (TOC), 'People are good,' underpins empathy. From a neuroscience perspective, empathy significantly impacts mental and emotional health. Neuroscientists argue that nurturing positive relationships can significantly influence well-being by enhancing brain function. Studies suggest that supportive, empathetic relationships stimulate the release of neurotransmitters like oxytocin and dopamine, which promote feelings of well-being and help regulate stress responses. They are also linked to lower rates of depression.

In summary, the benefits of fostering effective interactions with our loved ones in our workplace and socially extend beyond simply achieving collaboration and securing buy-in for implementing our plans.

Stage 6 - Ongoing Improvement Process

The process of ongoing improvement requires learning from experience. This stage of the MVS process suggests reviewing past experiences and achievements and identifying the next focus for improvement. Siegel mentions how learning with experience and discovering focus attention amplifies neuroplasticity by stimulating the release of neurochemicals that enhance the structural growth of synaptic linkages among activated neurons. (Siegel, The book Mindsight- The New Science of Personal Transformation)

The MVSystem, based on the TOC mindset, advocates for learning with experience during execution, facilitated by a 'fast feedback loop' to adapt behaviors, actions, and decision-making while respecting defined purposes and goals.

'Never say I know'; the fourth pillar of the Theory of Constraints (TOC) fosters our mindset to continuously grow and stretch our potential and brain's capacity to explore meaningful lives.

I confidently conclude that the TOC Mindset significantly impacts brain efficiency. By operating under the assumption that there are no limits to expanding our brain's potential, we embrace a process that encourages continuous learning and effectively harnessing the brain's capacity to rewire itself and enhance its power throughout our lives.

Finally, thinking clearly and acting with focus contribute to brain efficiency as we develop the following skills: one, simplify complex systems and define the focus to achieve meaningful goals; two, resolve dilemmas and generate win-win solutions, impacting the cortisol levels; three, develop effective personal interactions, avoiding stress and promoting the release of oxytocin; four, practice good habits to optimize brain capacity, mental and physical health;

five, eliminate distractions to enhance brain attention and productivity; six, expand limits, promoting a mindset of continuous growth... "Shall I continue to count?"

Throughout this book, we have explored the essence of the Theory of Constraints (TOC) and how its principles can be applied not only in the business environment but also in personal life to achieve significant and lasting growth. The journey we have shared is about understanding the inherent simplicity of complex systems and how to identify and overcome the constraints that prevent us from reaching our full potential.

Defining and living according to a clear purpose is fundamental to a meaningful life. Purpose provides direction, motivates our actions, and helps us face challenges with resilience and determination. When we know what we want to achieve, every step becomes more focused, and we make choices aligned with our beliefs and values.

TOC teaches us that every system, no matter how complex it may seem, possesses an inherent simplicity. By identifying and focusing on the main constraint, we can direct our efforts to where they will have the greatest impact. This principle applies not only to organizations but also to our personal lives. By understanding and addressing the root cause of our life contexts, we can transform our realities in a profound and lasting way.

Empathy is a prerequisite for persuasion and crucial in executing any change plan. Empathy allows us to understand others' assumptions more deeply to engage our ideas accordingly. Persuasion happens effectively to inspire others to join us on our journey. Together, these skills create an environment of collaboration and support essential for the success of any endeavor.

The MVSystem is a practical application of TOC principles for personal growth. It guides us through self-knowledge, purpose definition, planning, and focused execution. By following this method, we can transform our lives significantly.

This book's core is the belief that we all have the potential to live a full and meaningful life. TOC provides us with the tools and mindset needed to unlock that potential confidently and clearly.

Therefore, it is essential to recognize the legacy we leave behind by living a purposeful life. Each decision we make, each action we take, and each relationship we build contributes to our legacy. Living in alignment with our purpose not only enhances our own lives but also positively impacts the lives of those around us, creating a ripple effect of growth and fulfillment.

Each of us—whether as individuals, families, institutions, companies, or businesses—has the capability and potential to build a meaningful life. It all starts enhancing our ability to think.

May this book serve as a guide and inspiration for all those seeking to improve their lives. The journey to a meaningful life is not free of challenges, although there is hope when we know the process of how to overcome them. The process brings hope in achieving a life that is not only successful by conventional standards but deeply fulfilling and aligned with our true selves.

Embrace the process of thinking clearly and acting with focus. Allow yourself to dream, define your purpose, and take the necessary steps to bring that purpose to life. Remember that every system, including our lives, has an inherent simplicity waiting to be discovered and leveraged for our growth and happiness.

May the principles discussed here help you think clearly, act with focus, and live meaningfully. The journey to a more meaningful life begins with a simple step: the willingness to improve the way we think to foster the courage needed to move forward.

What matters is to ensure we're enjoying the journey for a significant reason. The results become evident and can exceed our expectations, lasting much longer than we might imagine.

Think clearly and act with focus – for a meaningful life!

REFERENCES

BORESS, Allan S. (1996). Odeio Vender. São Paulo, SP, Publisher McGraw-Hill Ltda.

BURCHARD, Brendon. (2012). The Charge. New York, NY, Publisher Free Press.

DWECK, Carol S. (2016). Mindset. Rio de Janeiro, RJ, Publisher Schwarcz.

GOLDRATT, Eliyahu M. The Goal. (2004). Great Barrington, MA, Publisher The North River Press.

GOLDRATT, Eliyahu M. & GOLDRATT, Efrat Ashlag. A Escolha. Barueri, SP, Publisher Nobel.

GOLEMAN, Daniel. (2014). Foco. Rio de Janeiro, RJ, Publisher Objetiva.

GOLEMAN, Daniel. (1995). Inteligência Emocional. Rio de Janeiro, RJ, Publisher Objetiva.

KELLER, Gary & PAPASAN, Jay. (2014). A Única Coisa. São Paulo, SP, Publisher Novo Século.

KOFMAN, Fred (2013). Conscious Business. Boulder, Colorado, Publisher Sounds True.

KOFMAN, Fred (2018). The Meaning Revolution. New York, NY, Publisher Currency.

LEVITIN, Daniel J. (2020). The Organized Mind. United States of America. Dutton.

MIT. (2024). Neuroscience for Business. Instructor: Tara Swart. Massachusetts Institute of Technology.

SELIGMAN, Martin E.P. (2002). Felicidade Autêntica. Rio de Janeiro, RJ, Publisher Objetiva.

SELIGMAN, Martin E.P. (1990). Aprenda a ser otimista. Rio de Janeiro, RJ, Publisher Objetiva.

SELIGMAN, Martin E.P. (2011). Florescer. Rio de Janeiro, RJ, Publisher Objetiva.

SIEGEL, Daniel J. M.D. (2011). Mindsight. United States of America. Bantam Books.

SWART, Tara (2019). The Source. London. Penguin Random House UK.